MW00994607

JOURNEYS OF THE APOSTLE PAUL

EDITED BY

DAVID BOMAR

Journeys of the Apostle Paul

Adapted with permission from content published in *Bible Study Magazine* (Volume 9, Issue 5; Volume 10, Issues 1, 3, 5; and Volume 11, Issue 5)

Lexham Press, 1313 Commercial St., Bellingham, WA 98225
LexhamPress.com

Print ISBN: 9781683593577
Library of Congress Control Number: 2019949169

Editor: David Bomar
Lexham editorial team: Jessi Strong, Derek R. Brown, Matthew Boffey, Erin Mangum
Art direction and cover design: Brittany Schrock
Interior design: Lydia Dahl

CONTENTS

FOREWORD

I first became drawn to the journeys of Paul as a teenager. My parents had given me a Thompson Chain-Reference Bible for my birthday—and though I had little interest in tracing chain references, I loved to study the maps and charts in the back. I still have this Bible, and I still consult the notes I made as a teenager to connect the chronology of Paul's journeys with the letters he wrote along the way.

On various segments of his travels, Paul was accompanied by a physician named Luke who, according to church tradition, recorded the events in the book of Acts. Luke portrays Paul as an apostle; the Greek word *apostolos* means "one who is sent." In Paul's case, he was sent by God to deliver a specific message to the gentiles, meaning anyone who was not part of God's chosen people, the Jews. In other words, God sent Paul to deliver a message for most of the world.

As the day-to-day realities of Paul's mission became clearer in my mind, I was captivated by the idea of this intensely driven Jewish man trekking around the Mediterranean world, encountering new cultures and boldly proclaiming that Israel's Messiah was the true king of the whole world. I could imagine why many of his listeners found him absurd. Yet if we trust Luke's account (and I do), Paul was successful in many respects. He left a legacy of Christian communities that perpetuated the gospel; of a church that welcomed all people into the family of God; of sound doctrine that has shaped the faith for two millennia.

My abiding interest in Paul's journeys and letters led to a five-part series of special sections in *Bible Study Magazine*. Between July 2017 and July 2018, we covered Paul's three missionary journeys and his voyage to Rome; in July 2019, we ended at the beginning, with a section on Paul's life-changing trip to Damascus. The articles from these magazine sections have been reedited and redesigned for the book you now hold.

In preparing this collection, I was struck by how many writers—without prompting—chose to emphasize Paul's ministry to the gentiles. This surely is a significant theme that receives too little attention in our efforts to learn from Paul. After all, most Christians qualify as gentiles, meaning we trace our spiritual heritage back through Paul. But more importantly, the gentile theme invites us to look forward. The sense that there are still outsiders to faith should propel our own missions.

In the book's closing piece on Rome, Craig Keener portrays Paul as a model for all Christians. So who are our "gentiles"? Who are the outsiders we are sent to? Who can we welcome into God's family?

David Bomar, editor

BREATHING THREATS & MURDER

Many of us are familiar with Paul because we've read or perhaps studied the letters he wrote. He is the most prominent writer in the New Testament, arguing forcefully for the gospel in Romans, instructing the church in Corinthians, and encouraging the believers in Philippians. As we read these and other letters, we come to see Paul's heart for sharing Christ with the world.

But before he was Paul the missionary/pastor/writer, he was Saul the persecutor. He first appears in the Bible at the end of Acts 7. The setting is near Jerusalem, perhaps within a year of Jesus' death and resurrection. Stephen, a leader among the Jerusalem Christians, has been falsely accused of speaking against God, and he is being stoned to death just outside the city. The witnesses to Stephen's execution "laid aside their coats at the feet of a young man named Saul" (Acts 7:58). The dark portrait of Saul becomes clearer in the opening lines of chapters 8 and 9: "Saul was agreeing with [Stephen's] murder. ... Saul was attempting to destroy the church. ... Saul, still breathing threats and murder against the disciples of the Lord" (Acts 8:1, 3; 9:1).

Who was this fierce opponent of the first Christians? And how should we understand his remarkable transformation into the leading missionary for Christ?

The answers are found on the Damascus road.

Julius Schnorr von Carolsfield, "The Stoning of Saint Stephen" (1852), for Die Bibel in Bildern

PROLOGUE

CRAIG S. KEENER

WHO WAS SAUL OF TARSUS?

Saul was from the Jewish tribe of Benjamin, and his parents gave him the name of the one ancient Benjamite king (*Shaul*). They may have chosen this name because its Greek form (*Saoul* or *Saoulos*) sounded similar to his Roman name, *Paulus*.

Contrary to what some people think, Saul did not change his name to Paul because of his conversion to Christian faith. He already had both names. But when he was among Greeks and Romans, it made sense for him to go by his Roman name. His Jewish name sounds like a Greek word that means "effeminate" and was used as an insult when referring to men. Outside Judea, Paul's Roman name would work much better!

CITIZEN OF ROME AND TARSUS

Saul was a Roman citizen by birth. The name *Paulus* (in English, Paul) was so rare for non-Romans (even rarer among Jews) that most people would have assumed his Roman-ness from his name. Citizenship gave Saul status in the eastern Mediterranean world, where, apart from Roman colonies, even most civic officials were not Roman citizens.

Although some scholars have questioned whether Jews like Saul could have Roman citizenship, ancient sources clearly indicate there were Jewish Roman citizens. How did Saul's ancestors acquire Roman citizenship? In the first century BC, a Roman general enslaved many Judeans. Later in Rome, other Jews bought the Jewish slaves' freedom. Adults properly freed by Roman citizens became Roman citizens themselves, called *libertini*. This meant Rome suddenly held many Jewish Roman citizens. Some of these *libertini* migrated eastward, especially during times of tension for Jews in Rome. For example, in the early first century AD, the emperor Tiberius expelled most Jews.

Saul's parents or ancestors settled in the city of Tarsus in Cilicia, and eventually his family moved to Jerusalem. There, they probably joined the "synagogue of the freedpersons," mentioned in Acts 6:9. This was a prestigious synagogue founded by *libertini,* and it included immigrants from Cilicia.

Paul attributes his good Greek—probably meaning his northern Mediterranean accent—to his earliest years in the city of Tarsus (Acts 21:37–39). Tarsus was the capital of Cilicia. It was a "free" city, meaning that Rome granted it some freedom to run its own affairs. A prominent trading city, Tarsus also was one of the most elite university centers during the first century AD, hosting many philosophers and orators.

Saul's family were Tarsian citizens. Tarsus did not grant this status to all Jews, but Saul's family was no ordinary family. Roman citizenship gave them some status

DRACHMA COIN

Creative Commons

by itself, and a family that could pay the esteemed rabbi Gamaliel to tutor their son (more on this below) was wealthy enough to purchase local citizenship. By the late first century, the price of citizenship in Tarsus was 500 drachmas (one drachma was roughly a day's wage for a laborer). Based on earlier practices, some scholars doubt that a person could be both a Tarsian citizen and a Roman one, but this was no longer true by Saul's day.

GALATIA

CILICIA

Saul's birthplace. He spent time here between his conversion and his first missionary journey (Acts 9:30; 22:3).

Tarsus

Antioch

After Saul became a Christian, the church here became his base for launching missionary journeys (Acts 13:1–3; 15:35–36; 18:22–23).

CYPRUS

SYRIA

MEDITERRANEAN SEA

Damascus

Christians fled here from Jerusalem, where Saul had been persecuting them (Acts 8:1–3; 9:1–2). Saul was in pursuit when the risen Jesus confronted him (9:1–5; 22:5–8; 26:12–15).

Saul probably moved here at a young age and was educated by a leading rabbi (Acts 22:3).

Jerusalem

JUDEA

RAISED IN JERUSALEM

Many Jews lived in Tarsus. They were loyal to Tarsus while also loyal to Judea, their ancestral homeland. Jewish adult males outside the holy land paid an annual tax for the upkeep of the temple. Each year, they would send local Jewish representatives to Jerusalem to deliver the tax. Jews of the **diaspora** counted it

> DIASPORA
>
> *Jewish people living outside the holy land are commonly described as "the diaspora"—a Greek word meaning "dispersion." In Acts 2:5–12, the Holy Spirit is poured out on members of the diaspora who were visiting Jerusalem.*

a special privilege to make pilgrimage to the Holy Land or eventually settle there. Greek-speaking Jews from the Mediterranean world who migrated to the Holy Land would naturally settle especially in Jerusalem or on the coast, where many people spoke Greek and a critical mass of foreign Jews had settled.

Like other Jewish boys outside the Holy Land, Saul would have started learning the Jewish scriptures (the Old Testament) at a young age, probably by oral memorization. As a faithful Jew, he also would have attended the local synagogue,

> PHARISEES
>
> *The Pharisees were a Jewish party that practiced strict piety according to the law of Moses. For more on the Pharisees, see page 11.*
>
> *Miguel Manrique, "The Magdalene anointing the Feet of Christ, or Dinner at Levi's House" (c. 1647)*

where he heard the law of Moses read and interpreted. But Saul's primary training came in Jerusalem, the capital of Jewish learning. Many Tarsians studied abroad, but Saul's entire family probably settled in Jerusalem when he was young.

Ancient writers often distinguished a person's birth, upbringing, and training. In Acts 22:3, Paul says he was "born" in Tarsus, but "brought up" and "educated" in Jerusalem. This depicts three phases of his background, probably suggesting that he spent most of his young life in Jerusalem. Other details seem to confirm this: in Acts 23:6, Paul says his father was a **Pharisee**—and Pharisees were rare outside the holy land; in Acts 23:16, we hear of Paul's nephew in Jerusalem, which suggests his extended family lived in the vicinity. A Judean upbringing also fits what Paul writes in Galatians 1:14 about his advancement in Judaism and his zeal for ancestral traditions.

Whereas adults often find it difficult to learn a new language, children often quickly pick up the local language while also speaking their family one. Saul's upbringing in Jerusalem helps explain his skill in the local Judean language, mentioned in Acts 21:40 and 22:2. Although the Greek text doesn't specify which language, it probably was Aramaic, which is closely related to Hebrew. In Philippians 3:5, Paul writes that he was a "Hebrew of Hebrews."

ADVANCED STUDY WITH GAMALIEL

In his training, Saul quickly advanced among his peers and apparently achieved leadership while still young (Galatians 1:14; Acts 7:58). Ancient sources depict such men as prodigies, as admirable exceptions to the norm of leadership by elders. What did Saul study? Whereas educated Greeks displayed their learning with abundant classical quotations, Paul's letters betray instead advanced training in the Jewish scriptures.

Saul's family had settled in the ideal location for this training. Advanced and financially wealthy students might study rhetoric in Alexandria or medicine in

TORAH

The Hebrew word torah *means "instruction," but it also can refer to the Jewish law and to the first five books of the Old Testament.*

Restored Torah scroll from the Glockengasse Synagogue in Cologne, Germany

Pergamum, but the best place to study the **Torah** was Judea—and the best place in Judea for a Greek-speaking Jew to study the Torah was Jerusalem.

Saul would, of course, receive some other instruction at this advanced level, perhaps including further exposure to Greek rhetoric (the study of using language to be persuasive). We might compare this to a Bible major who took a few preaching courses. In later years, Paul certainly shows his rhetorical skills in debate settings and in his letters.

Advancing beyond his peers undoubtedly included studying with a prominent teacher, so it is no surprise that Saul studied with a rabbi and Pharisee named Gamaliel. The Jewish ruling council, called the Sanhedrin, was probably dominated by the Pharisees' frequent rivals, the Sadducees. Nevertheless, Gamaliel was so prominent that, even as a Pharisee, he became a leading member of the Sanhedrin. Acts 5:34 describes Gamaliel as "respected by all the people."

There were two schools of Pharisees: the followers of the rabbi Shammai were more strict in their interpretation of the Jewish law, while Pharisees who followed the rabbi Hillel were more tolerant. Gamaliel belonged to the school of Hillel, and his tendency toward tolerance is reflected in Acts 5:33–39. After Peter and other apostles teach about Jesus, the Sanhedrin is infuriated—even considering executing the apostles. Amid the furor, Gamaliel persuades the ruling council to take a wait-and-see approach. If the Christian apostles are false, he says, they will be overthrown; but if they are from God, we should not oppose them.

The school of Hillel was in the minority during the early first century, but any Pharisee would have wanted to study with this prestigious teacher. The fact that

Saul was able to do so implies that his family had considerable resources. In Acts 22:3, he says he was brought up "at the feet of Gamaliel," referring to the ideal posture for disciples. Because Gamaliel was a Pharisee, studying under him would include learning not only the Jewish scriptures but also the ancestral traditions, which Pharisees passed down meticulously. According to ancient sources, Gamaliel's household trained some students in Greek language and literature. Saul's focus was apparently the Septuagint, the dominant Greek version of the Old Testament. His New Testament letters reveal an awareness of the differences between the Hebrew and Greek versions of the Jewish scriptures. His letters also demonstrate his phenomenal memory of the Septuagint—the scriptures used by his diaspora audiences.

Disciples of rabbis were usually in their teens. (Once boys reached puberty, they were considered adults and thus could travel independently.) Despite exceptions, even most wealthy students finished their education and began their public careers by age 18. So Saul had likely finished his formal instruction by the time he began persecuting Christians. In contrast to his tolerant teacher Gamaliel, Saul would learn the hard way that resisting God is futile.

NATIONALISTIC ZEAL

Paul associates his persecution of Jesus' followers with his zeal for preserving Jewish traditions (Acts 22:3–4; Galatians 1:13–14; Philippians 3:6). During the first century AD, many young Judeans, including Pharisees, pursued the nationalistic model of zeal offered by **the Maccabees**, who drove out foreigners and executed apostates (Jews who seemed to be unfaithful to Yahweh). The Maccabees, in turn, were inspired by the Old Testament example of Phinehas, who saved the Israelites from God's wrath when he zealously killed an apostate (Numbers 25:11).

THE MACCABEES

During the second century BC, Judea was ruled by the Seleucid Empire, which at one point demanded that Jews abandon their traditions and adopt pagan practices. Jewish resistors led by Judas "Maccabeus" (a nickname meaning "the hammer") mounted a widespread rebellion in 167–160 BC. They later came to be called the Maccabees. Their story is recorded in the book of 1 Maccabees (which isn't included in most Protestant Bibles).

Wojciech Korneli Stattler, "Maccabees" (1842)

PERSECUTING JESUS' FOLLOWERS BECAME SAUL'S PERSONAL CRUSADE.

Saul probably understood his zeal in similar terms. In Galatians 1:13–14, he writes:

For you have heard about my former way of life in Judaism, that to an extraordinary degree I was persecuting the church of God, and trying to destroy it, and was progressing in Judaism beyond many contemporaries in my nation, because I was a far more zealous adherent of the traditions handed down by my forefathers. (ESV)

In the first century AD, the term usually translated "Judaism" in Galatians 1:13–14 apparently meant not simply Jewish faith or heritage, but Judean nationalism and hostility to foreign customs.

What apparently mobilizes Saul's crusade against Jesus' followers is the (false) charge against Stephen. By allegedly speaking against the holy temple and ancestral customs, Stephen, a fellow Greek-speaking Jew, seemed to oppose everything Saul stood for. Indeed, judging from his speech in Acts 7, Stephen counted even places outside the holy land as holy, relativizing the temple!

Saul began persecuting Christians while a "young man" (Acts 7:58). The Greek term here (*neanias*) can refer to anyone from his teens through age 40, but Saul was probably in his late teens or early 20s when Stephen was killed. Saul's role seems prominent: those executing Stephen left their cloaks at Saul's feet, just as believers left resources at the apostles' feet (4:35). In other words, by the time Stephen was killed, Saul had already achieved leadership in the movement to persecute Jesus' followers.

In Acts 26:10, Paul says he cast his "vote" against Stephen. This does not mean, however, that Saul was a member of the Sanhedrin, as some interpreters have thought. The Sanhedrin's members were mostly older. Greek writers often apply the image of casting a vote figuratively, to mean showing approval. At least sometimes, as here, they do so in a wordplay. The Greek word *psephos,* normally translated in verse 10 as "vote," can also mean "pebble," and pebbles were often used for voting. So while the (false) witnesses are casting stones, Saul casts his pebble.

Persecuting Jesus' followers became Saul's personal crusade. Acts 8:3 explains that he arrested not only men but also women, which was less common in his day. Saul was from a sufficiently prominent family to secure an audience with the high priest, Caiaphas. Acts 9:1–2 describes Saul asking Caiaphas for letters of recommendation to synagogues in Damascus. Saul was planning to arrest Jewish followers of Jesus in Damascus who had fled his repression in Jerusalem.

But Saul was about to be arrested by someone else instead—someone who would harness his zeal for a *genuinely* divine purpose. The defender of Judean heritage, the opponent of foreign customs, would soon be sent to gentiles as an apostle of Israel's Messiah.

BACKDROPS

CARYN A. REEDER

WHO WERE THE PHARISEES?

Paul's autobiography in Philippians 3:4–6 gives us a rare firsthand perspective on the Pharisees in the first century AD. We otherwise hear about the Pharisees from outsiders—such as the Gospel writers or the Jewish historian Josephus, who wrote in the late first century.[1] But Paul himself belonged to the Pharisees, and he highlights three of their important concerns: Jewish identity, the law, and zeal.

First, Paul says he is fully Jewish by both ancestry and circumcision. Some Jews were gentile converts: "proselytes" were committed to keeping the law of Moses (including circumcision), while "God-fearers" worshiped God without adopting the entire Jewish law. But in Philippians, Paul suggests that being Jewish by birth was valuable and important to him before he became a follower of Jesus. Jews in the first century found different ways to maintain their Jewish identity in a world ruled

LIVING BY THE LAW WAS A WAY FOR THE PHARISEES TO PARTICIPATE IN GOD'S SALVATION.

by **gentiles**. The Pharisees emphasized ancestral traditions. Unlike their main rivals, the wealthy and powerful Sadducees, the Pharisees rejected the luxuries of Greco-Roman culture and refused to swear loyalty to Herod the Great and the Romans.[2] At least some Pharisees were involved in the rebellions against

> GENTILES
>
> *In the Bible, the term "gentile" simply refers to someone who is not Jewish. From the perspective of most Jews, gentiles were outsiders who didn't belong in God's holy people.*

Rome in the first century.[3] They were Israel-centric, looking for the restoration of Israel as a nation under God.

Jewish identity relates to Paul's second focus, the law. The law was God's gift to Israel, so the people of God could be holy as God is holy (Deuteronomy 26:16–19). Anyone familiar with the Gospels knows that the Pharisees were enthusiastic students, practitioners, and teachers of the law. We might be tempted to dismiss the Pharisees' focus on the law as legalistic, or as an impossible burden. However, Paul himself says he was righteous and blameless according to the law—which implies living by the law was possible. Moreover, obedience to the law gained extra importance from the hope for national restoration. The Bible promises that, when the Israelites are sent into exile as punishment for breaking the covenant, God will restore them when they repent and return to faithful obedience (Deuteronomy 30:1–10). Living by the law—and teaching others to keep the law—was a way for the Pharisees to participate in God's salvation.

The Pharisees were very interested in Jesus. Some Pharisees, including Paul, became followers of Jesus themselves. But most Pharisees felt threatened by Jews who didn't observe ancestral traditions—people like Jesus, who broke the Sabbath; Stephen, who challenged the very heart of Jewish identity; and Peter, who ate with uncircumcised gentiles. Paul's own zeal for God drove him to persecute Jesus' followers in Jerusalem and beyond. The Pharisees sought to protect Israel's identity as the faithful, covenant people of God both in their practice and teaching of the law and in their violence against lawbreakers.

The Gospels record many debates and conflicts between the Pharisees and Jesus and his disciples. To some extent, that hostility comes from similarities between the two groups. Just like Jesus' followers, the Pharisees expected the messiah, the kingdom of God, and the resurrection of the dead. But Jesus brought an unexpected kingdom—one that welcomed the "unclean" and "sinners," collaborators with Roman rule (the tax collectors), and even gentiles. To the Pharisees, this message threatened to undermine the Jews' faithfulness to their covenant with God.[4]

BACKDROPS

CARYN A. REEDER

WHO WERE THE CHRISTIANS SAUL PERSECUTED?

If we had the chance to visit a church in the first century AD, we might not recognize it. Instead of a Sunday morning program, Christians met frequently throughout the week. They gathered in homes, marketplaces, and colonnades along the street. There were no worship leaders or pastors; everyone was welcome to share a story or teaching, a prayer, a song, food, and material resources. Our first-century sisters and brothers would likely find us to be pretty strange, too. What do we mean by "going to church," for instance? The church is the living body of Christ. It is not a destination, but "the Way"—the name given to the early Christian movement in Acts (9:2; 24:14).

AT COMMUNITY GATHERINGS, CHRISTIANS CHALLENGED EACH OTHER TO IMITATE JESUS.

Despite our differences, the essential identity of the church as a missional community has not changed. In Acts 1:8, Jesus charges the disciples to be his witnesses from Jerusalem to the ends of the earth. The rest of Acts and the New Testament letters tell the story of Jesus' followers on the move, announcing the gospel of Jesus—especially the victory of his death and resurrection. The New Testament tells the story of the spread of the church from Jerusalem to Rome. Unfortunately, we don't know much about the early missions to the south or east (Egypt and North Africa, Syria, Persia, or beyond).

The mission was at first Jewish. The earliest followers of Jesus were all Jewish, and they bore witness to Jesus in the temple in Jerusalem, the very heart of Judaism. They lived according to the law of Moses and worshiped in the temple. James, the head of the Jerusalem church (and brother of Jesus), was renowned for his faithful, righteous piety.[1]

Even when the followers of Jesus left Jerusalem to preach the gospel elsewhere, their primary audience remained the Jews. However, church communities slowly incorporated gentiles. At first, they welcomed God-fearers like Cornelius who were already interested in Judaism, such as Cornelius in Acts 10. Then people from pagan backgrounds began to join the church.

At the end of Peter's speech to the Jewish pilgrims in Jerusalem at Pentecost, he calls them to repent. Those who do are baptized as a mark of their new identity. They promptly "devoted themselves to the apostles' teaching and fellowship, to the breaking of bread and to prayer" (Acts 2:42 NRSV). These four activities reflect the practice of the church across the New Testament.

The apostles—men and women who had known Jesus and could witness to his words and actions (especially his resurrection)—passed their stories on to others. At community gatherings, Christians told stories about Jesus, discussed the Jewish scriptures (our Old Testament), talked about God's work in the world, and challenged each other to imitate Jesus. They prayed together. They sang the psalms—and perhaps also new songs about Jesus.[2]

The word "fellowship" in Acts 2:42 is translating the Greek word *koinonia,* an idea that reflects the common identity of the followers of Jesus. Shared meals—both the Lord's supper and potluck-style feasts—represent *koinonia* as a sign of hospitality, welcome, and relationship. Fellowship also meant sharing each other's burdens, providing for brothers and sisters in need locally and in other cities.[3]

The different communities of Jesus' followers in the first century were one *koinonia,* bound together by their fellowship as the body of Christ. We are part of the same *koinonia,* carrying on their mission of bearing witness about Jesus to the ends of the earth.

THE ROAD TO DAMASCUS | ACTS 9:1–22

JOSEPH R. DODSON

A NEW HOPE & A DIVINE DIRECTION

CONFRONTED BY ORACLES, THE PERSECUTOR BECAME AN APOSTLE

A long time ago in a country far, far away, I was reading Acts 9 to my children for their bedtime story. In this pivotal chapter of Acts, the apostle Paul experiences a life-changing message that transforms his views about God and sets the trajectory of his gospel ministry.

When I got to the part where the Lord tells Ananias that Paul would become the apostle to the gentiles, my son Kinnon interrupted me. Being far too obsessed with "Star Wars" for a 6-year-old, Kinnon—whom we now appropriately call "Kenobi"—blurted: "Oh, oh, oh! Like the prophecy from Qui-Gon Jinn about how Anakin Skywalker is going to bring balance to the Force!" He kept rambling. Not wanting to rain on his Jedi parade, I replied, "Yeah, kinda, I guess. Maybe," and then went on with my story. In retrospect, however, perhaps Kenobi was on to something.

Prophetic oracles aren't just in the Bible or "Star Wars"; they also pepper ancient narratives, treatises, biographies, and speeches. In these writings, the utterances were often designed to be foggy, pregnant, vague, and misunderstood. This tended to hook audiences by making them curious as to how exactly the loaded words will come to pass.[1] Readers, however, were trained to expect the oracle to unfold in surprising ways (such as the shocking manner in which Anakin and Paul actually fulfill their respective prophecies).

THE PROMISE THAT PAUL WAS TO SUFFER TURNED OUT TO BE A SIGN: GOD HAD CHOSEN HIM FOR A SPECIAL PURPOSE.

A prime example from the ancient world involves an oracle about Socrates. When Socrates was 40 years old, a friend told him about an utterance he had received from the high priestess of Apollo: "No man is wiser than Socrates."[2] On hearing this, Socrates went on a quest to challenge the oracle. Surely heaven was mistaken, he thought. There was so much he didn't know. But how could the gods ever be wrong? In his search, he finally found a politician who was purported to be even smarter than Socrates. Therefore, he eagerly approached the man but soon walked away frustrated and dismayed. He had instantly realized he was, in fact, wiser than the politician—who, according to Socrates, was hardly as wise as he claimed. To be sure, the man knew how much he knew, but he did not—like Socrates—realize how much he didn't know. The oracle, then, had led Socrates to a transformational epiphany, his famous paradox of wisdom. "I am wise," Socrates inferred, because "I do not think I know what I do not know."

In ancient literature, divine oracles could be communicated through extraordinary sounds from heaven and by flashes of fire in the sky. More often, though, the gods spoke to people through visions, prophecies, and dreams. The function of these oracles was (1) to affirm certain actions of a character or to declare the figure as faithful and just. Moreover, an oracle could (2) encourage or warn individuals in the story; (3) explain incredible happenings; or (4) foreshadow and foretell future events.

PROPHETIC ORACLES IN PAUL'S LIFE & LETTERS

As Luke relates the history of the early church in Acts, he often incorporates common literary elements of his day, drawing from both the Old Testament and ancient literature. As the narrative unfolds, we see the Lord communicating in the life of Paul through oracles for exactly the reasons mentioned above.[3] For example, according to Acts, a light brighter than the sun flashed from heaven, and the Lord's voice thundered from the sky telling Paul to get up and go into Damascus to await further instructions.[4] Luke goes on to pair Paul's message with another one given to Ananias:

> *"Go! This man is my chosen instrument to proclaim my name to the Gentiles and their kings and to the people of Israel. I will show him how much he must suffer for my name." (Acts 9:15–16)*[5]

This utterance is fleshed out through the remainder of Acts and provides the dominating oracle for the second half of the book. The utterance also contains three threads that are foundational for Paul's letters: (1) the rocky relationship between his ministry to his fellow Jews and his outreach to the gentiles; (2) his opportunity to preach before rulers and kings; and (3) his call to suffer for the gospel.[6] Each of these threads, foretold in the oracle to Ananias, becomes a major theme of Paul's ministry.

TO THE GENTILES AND THE JEWS

Both Paul's compassion for his fellow Jews and his call to the gentiles are obvious from the start of his journey. In Acts 13, he sets off with Barnabas and begins to preach to Jews and gentiles. However, as soon as the non-believing Jews start to revile Paul and contradict his message, he surprisingly proclaims that even though it was necessary to preach to the Jews first, he will now turn to the gentiles.

To explain this seemingly rash decision, Paul shares another word he had received from the Lord:

> *"'I have made you a light for the Gentiles,*
> *that you may bring salvation to the ends of the earth.'"*
> *(Acts 13:47, paraphrasing Isaiah 49:6)*

In Acts 9, the oracle to Ananias appears to treat Paul's commissions equally: he will proclaim the Lord's name to the gentiles as well as to the Jews. But in Acts 13, the Lord's word to Paul stresses the mission to the gentiles and conspicuously omits a call to the Jews. The prophetic oracle of Acts 9 comes to fruition, then, in a remarkable way as the events play out in Acts 13: the people of Israel reject Paul's message about their promised Messiah, while in stark contrast many of the gentiles rejoice at and accept the good news about Israel's Christ.

This pattern continues through the rest of Acts. Although Paul will still offer the gospel to the Jews first, he often ends up quickly turning to the gentiles instead. What is more, this sequence serves as the culmination of the entire book. In the concluding chapter of Acts, Paul rages against the unbelieving Jews for not accepting Jesus and leaves them with some blistering parting words—a final oracle that anticipates how the two groups will receive the gospel beyond the book of Acts. Paul says to the unbelieving Jews:

> *"The Holy Spirit spoke the truth to your ancestors when he said through Isaiah the prophet:*
>
> *'Go to this people and say,*
> *"You will be ever hearing but never understanding;*
> *you will be ever seeing but never perceiving."*
> *For this people's heart has become calloused;*
> *they hardly hear with their ears, and they have closed their eyes.'...*
>
> *Therefore I want you to know that God's salvation has been sent to the Gentiles, and they will listen!" (Acts 28:25–28)*

The emphasis regarding Paul's focus on the gentiles also shows up in his letters. As early as Galatians, Paul writes how the leaders in the Jerusalem church acknowledged him as the one who was called to the gentiles just as Peter was called to the Jews (Galatians 2:7–9). And although Paul never gives up hope for Israel, he prides himself on being "the apostle to the gentiles" who was set apart to call these non-Jews to the obedience that comes from Abraham's faith (for example, see Romans 1:5; 4:16; 11:13).

BEFORE TWO KINGS

The second thread in Ananias' oracle is that Paul would proclaim the gospel before kings. For Luke's first-century audience, this prediction would have struck their curiosity: *what* kings will Paul stand before, and *how* will he get the opportunity to do so?

In the narrative of Acts, Paul appears before only one king—Herod Agrippa, the so-called king of Jews (see Acts 25–26). But a later oracle given to Paul clarifies the plural "kings" from Acts 9. Amid a fierce storm during his voyage to Rome, an angel tells Paul not to be afraid. He will not die at sea since he "must stand trial before Caesar" (27:24). The word comes true: Paul survives a shipwreck, a snakebite, and the final leg of the trip so that he eventually winds up in Rome waiting to appear before Nero, the dark lord of the empire.

Furthermore, Luke's audience might have been startled to find that Paul would come to stand trial before Herod and Caesar because his own people attempted to assassinate him. Therefore, in a twist for the audience, it is *in chains* that Paul witnesses to the kings. Moreover, this period of captivity was the setting in which Paul penned powerful letters such as Ephesians, Philippians, Colossians, and Philemon.

IN SUFFERING FOR THE GOSPEL

Also true to the Acts 9 oracle, Paul's ministry was replete with suffering. On his first missionary journey, Jewish leaders stirred up persecution that resulted in Paul being expelled from Pisidia, chased out of Iconium, and stoned in Lystra. Moreover, he was beaten and imprisoned in Philippi, seized and tried in Corinth, and nearly assassinated in Jerusalem. This is not even to mention the book's cliffhanger: Acts sharply concludes with Paul under house arrest in Rome, leaving the reader in suspense to ponder his fate.

Nevertheless, these encounters taught Paul that suffering and glory go hand in hand. Perhaps this paradox helps clarify the Acts 9 oracle. The promise that Paul was to suffer turned out to be a blessing, not a curse. Rather than a wrathful punishment, it was a sign that God had chosen Paul for a special purpose. Suffering was, for Paul, the necessary wound that grace must give before it can heal. As the initial oracle came to fruition in Paul's life, it proved the truths he later proclaimed in his letters—regarding how affliction produces perseverance, character, and hope; how he could endure all things through Christ who strengthens him; and how, in every situation, God's grace is altogether sufficient.

According to Paul, though, he is not the only one called to suffer for the gospel. This thread of the oracle also extends to us. In one of his first letters, Paul tells the believers not to be shaken by their afflictions because they, too, were destined for them (1 Thessalonians 3:3). And in his last letter, he proclaims that anyone who desires to live a godly life will be persecuted (2 Timothy 3:12).

The unfolding of that first oracle probably led Paul to the conviction that, like him, believers share in Christ's suffering so that they also may share in his glory (Romans 8:17). Just as Socrates' oracle led him to the paradox that when I am humble I am wise, Paul discovered that when we are weak, then we are strong (2 Corinthians 12:10).

THE ROAD TO DAMASCUS | ACTS 9:1–22

MATTHEW D. AERNIE

TRANSFORMED BY THE MESSIAH

HOW THE DAMASCUS ROAD EVENT SHAPED PAUL'S MINISTRY

Paul's encounter with the risen Lord Jesus on the Damascus road forever changed the course of his life and would make a permanent impact on the church. As a conversion experience, this event radically transformed Paul's understanding of Jesus Christ, whom he now confessed as his Lord. In addition, the Damascus road event resulted in Paul's specific calling to be the apostle to the gentiles.

But how, exactly, did Paul's conversion/call impact the ministry that would consume him for the rest of his life? To answer this question, we can explore three areas reflected in Acts and in Paul's letters: his theological framework, his prophetic self-understanding, and his views about the end times (eschatology).[1]

A THEOLOGICAL U-TURN

Prior to his conversion, Paul was "zealous for the traditions of his ancestors" (Galatians 1:14).[2] He was a dedicated Pharisee, a devout monotheist, and a faithful upholder of Old Testament teachings (Philippians 3:5–6). However, after his conversion, Paul came to understand his entire theological framework through the lens of faith in Christ. His understanding of Jesus Christ was radically changed, for he now understood Jesus to be the Son of God, the Savior of his people.

God graciously enabled Paul to understand that Jesus was both Lord and Messiah—the one who had fulfilled all of God's covenant promises and inaugurated the new-covenant era. This divine revelation transformed how Paul thought about the progression of God's redemptive work throughout history. It also completely reversed the focus of Paul's life, which would now be dedicated to proclaiming the good news of the risen Lord Jesus Christ.

The repercussions of this theological reorientation are evident throughout Paul's writings. He had built his life on the foundational precepts of Judaism—the law, circumcision, Sabbath, justification, sanctification, the people of God, the kingdom of God, redemption, atonement, the coming day of the Lord, and so on. Paul did not abandon these precepts, but he now interpreted them through what Christ had accomplished in his life, death, and resurrection.

A PROPHETIC CALLING

Although Paul never explicitly calls himself a prophet, scholars have long recognized numerous parallels between his divine appointment and the calling of the Old Testament prophets.[3] Indeed, Paul's commissioning on the Damascus road arguably bears many similarities to the callings of Moses, Isaiah, Jeremiah, and Ezekiel. Some of the more commonly observed parallels include:

- the prophet experiencing a **theophany**;
- the prophet declaring his unworthiness or inadequacies;
- the Lord overcoming the prophet's inadequacies and enabling him to carry out the ministry;
- the Lord giving the prophet a divine message; and
- the Lord granting the prophet authority to carry out the ministry.[4]

In his writings, Paul seems to indicate that he interpreted his divine appointment to be in line with the callings of the Old Testament prophets. For instance, in Galatians 1:15–16 Paul uses language reminiscent of the prophetic callings—particularly of Isaiah and Jeremiah—when he says that God had set him apart, called him by his grace, and appointed him as the apostle to the gentiles (see Isaiah 49:1–6; Jeremiah 1:5). He also mentions in Galatians 1:16a that "God

> THEOPHANY *A visible appearance of God.*
>
> CHRISTOPHANY *A visible appearance of Christ.*

had revealed his Son to me," which is arguably a reference to the **Christophany** he experienced on the Damascus road. Paul may be indicating that the risen Lord had appeared to him physically, not just in the heavenly light and voice described in Acts 9:4–6.

A further example involves passages where Paul recognizes his insufficiencies and understands that only by God's grace can he carry out his new-covenant ministry. Just as Moses, Isaiah, and Jeremiah all recognized their inadequacies, Paul affirmed his insufficiency and acknowledged his dependence on God's grace and power.[5] This is why he can say "whenever I am weak, then I am strong" (2 Corinthians 12:10).

The outcome of the Damascus road event was that Paul interpreted his new-covenant ministry to correspond with the ministry of the Old Testament prophets. Granted, Paul's *message* was distinct from the messages of the

Old Testament prophets, in that he preached repentance and faith in Jesus Christ. But Paul's *mission* was the same. Just like those prophets, he faithfully proclaimed the message God had given him.

A NEW VISION OF FINAL JUDGMENT

In the Old Testament, Yahweh sometimes manifests himself or "comes down" in various forms to confront his people regarding judgment and salvation. Paul seems to have recognized the parallels between these Old Testament theophanies and his own Christophany on the Damascus road. For instance, he reminds the Corinthians that he had seen the Lord and tells the Galatians that God was pleased to reveal his Son to him (1 Corinthians 9:1; Galatians 1:16).

Paul was certainly familiar with Old Testament teachings about the "day of the Lord"—when God would ultimately judge his enemies and vindicate his people. In theological scholarship, the term for this area of study is "eschatology" (the Greek word *eschaton* means "final event"). On the Damascus road, Paul's eschatological framework was reoriented; he was confronted with the reality that the final Judge will be none other than risen Lord Jesus. For Paul, the Damascus road Christophany was, in essence, a preview of the day of the Lord.

Paul had once believed it was his duty before God to extinguish the new movement that was proclaiming a crucified and risen Messiah. But the pursuer was actually being pursued. And when the risen Christ appeared, he pronounced a severe indictment against Paul—namely that he was guilty of fighting against God (Acts 9:4–5; 26:14). This accusation forced Paul to realize that he actually stood guilty before the Judge of all the earth. But even as Paul stood condemned, having no defense, the Judge granted him mercy, transformed his life, and appointed him with a new vocation.

This Christophany radically altered how Paul understood God's plan for judging and redeeming the world, which in turn shaped his approach to ministry. He was confronted with the fact that the Son of God functions as the Father's judicial agent, to whom all people must give an account. He realized that the day of the Lord was more imminent than ever before and that "the time is short ... for the present shape of this world is passing away" (1 Corinthians 7:29–31).

The reality of the return of Christ and the consummation of all things meant there was an urgency in Paul's missionary work. For instance, when he writes "now is the day of salvation" (2 Corinthians 6:2), he means that God is presently at work redeeming his people through his Son. But when the Father completes his work of reconciliation, the day of the Lord will commence and Christ will come to render judgments.

Like the Old Testament prophets who preceded him, Paul proclaimed that the final day of the Lord will be a day of both vindication and condemnation: vindication for those who identify with Christ by faith, and condemnation for those who reject him.

Paul's life was radically transformed when he saw the risen Lord Jesus. At one moment he was working *against* the Messiah, and in the next he was working *for* the Messiah. Seeing Jesus on the Damascus road reversed the trajectory of Paul's life, resulting in a ministry that would have a lasting impact on the church.

Mitylene

Smyrna

Athens

Ephesus

Corinth

ACHAIA

Miletus

CRETE

PAUL'S FIRST MISSIONARY JOURNEY

GALATIA

CA

Pisidian Antioch

Acts 13:13–50, 14:21
Setting for Paul's first recorded sermon (see page 38).

Acts 13:51–14:5, 14:21
Paul and Barnabas stay here for a long time, boldly preaching the gospel and demonstrating its power. Many Jews and gentiles become believers, but many others stir up opposition to the apostles, forcing them to flee.

Iconium

Lystra

Acts 13:13–14; 14:25
On the return trip, the apostles preach in this provincial capital.

Acts 14:6–21
After witnessing the gospel's healing power, the citizens here think Paul and Barnabas are Zeus and Hermes (see page 42).

Derbe

Attalia

Perga

Acts 14:6–7, 20
The turnaround point on the first journey. The apostles make many disciples here.

Tarsu

The city where

Salamis

CYPRUS

Paphos

Acts 13:4–12
See pages 30, 34.

MEDITERRANEAN SEA

Acts
After
Jerusa
discus
comm

J

JUDEA

PPADOCIA

CILICIA

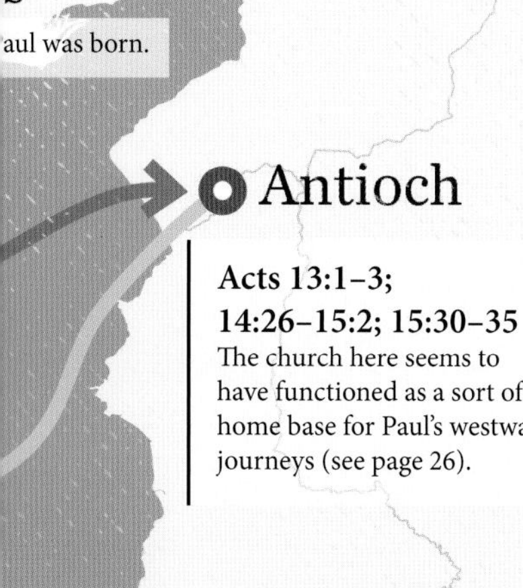
S
aul was born.
Antioch
Acts 13:1–3;
14:26–15:2; 15:30–35
The church here seems to
have functioned as a sort of
home base for Paul's westward
journeys (see page 26).

SYRIA

15:4–29
ıe first journey, Paul and Barnabas visit the
em church leaders to report on their ministry and
the status of gentile Christians. This episode is
ɔnly called the "Jerusalem Council" (see page 50).

erusalem

Paul's Travel Companions on the First Missionary Journey

Acts indicates that a number of people traveled with Paul on the first missionary journey, but the text names only two: Barnabas and John Mark.

Barnabas

"Barnabas" ("son of encouragement") was the nickname the apostles gave to Joseph, a prominent member of the early church. He was a Levite from the island of Cyprus. He apparently was a man of means, since he was able to sell a piece of land and give the money to the apostles (Acts 4:36–37).

After Paul went from persecuting the church to following Christ, the Christian leaders in Jerusalem were hesitant to trust him. It was Barnabas who smoothed things out, bringing Paul before the apostles and vouching for the authenticity of his conversion (Acts 9:27).

The church in Jerusalem sent Barnabas to minister to the growing number of gentile believers in Antioch. Luke reports that he "was a good man and full of the Holy Spirit and of faith" and that "a large number were added to the Lord" through his ministry (Acts 11:24). Barnabas brought Paul from Tarsus to Antioch, and they ministered together there for a year.

Barnabas joined Paul only on the first missionary journey. Just before the second journey, they had a falling out and went separate ways—Barnabas to Cyprus and Paul to Asia Minor.

John Mark

In first-century Palestine, men commonly went by a Hebrew name with family and friends and a Greek or Roman name in the wider community. Acts 12:25 and 15:37 clarify that "John" (Hebrew) was also called "Mark" (Roman); other references use one name or the other. Once the connection is made, it appears that John Mark was Barnabas' cousin (Colossians 4:10).

John Mark's mother hosted a gathering of Christians at her house in Jerusalem. When Paul and Barnabas sailed from Antioch to Cyprus, they took John Mark with them as a helper. But when they left Cyprus for Perga, John Mark went to Jerusalem. Paul viewed this as a desertion and subsequently refused to bring John Mark on the second missionary journey; this prompted Barnabas to part ways with Paul and travel instead to Cyprus with John Mark.

Whatever rift might have existed between Paul and John Mark seems to have been reconciled by the writing of Colossians, which identifies "Mark, the cousin of Barnabas," among Paul's "fellow workers" who had provided him comfort (Colossians 4:10–11). Other letters attributed to Paul speak favorably about a "Mark" who might be the same person (2 Timothy 4:11; Philemon 24).

In addition, the John Mark of Acts might have been acquainted with Peter (Acts 12:12–17), and church tradition since around AD 110–150 has identified John Mark as the author of Mark's Gospel.

Compiled from Lexham Bible Dictionary

THE FIRST MISSIONARY JOURNEY & THE JERUSALEM COUNCIL

ACTS 13:1–15:35

A LIGHT TO THE GENTILES

We often think of Paul as a theologian and writer—as the apostle whose letters established key teachings of the Christian faith. But Paul did much more than think and write.

In the decades after Jesus' death and resurrection, Paul planted churches throughout the northeastern Mediterranean region. His missionary work led to countless Christian converts, and he experienced miraculous displays of God's power. He also encountered stiff resistance at times, leading to imprisonments and beatings.

In the essays that follow, we explore each episode of Paul's initial westward journey, from Syria to Cyprus to Galatia. We also consider Paul's subsequent visit to Jerusalem, where he met with Christian leaders to discuss the status of gentiles in the church. The narrative accounts of these trips, found in Acts 13–15, depict the gospel's steady advance beyond Jerusalem and other Jewish communities in the region. Paul and his companions were committed to taking the good news about Jesus into places where pagan deities and the Roman emperor were worshiped.

According to Acts 13:47, Paul and Barnabas identified their missionary calling in the prophecy of Isaiah: "For so the Lord has commanded us, saying, 'I have set you to be a light for the gentiles, so that you may bring salvation to the ends of the earth'" (quoting Isaiah 49:6). To pursue this mission, Paul abandoned everything and embraced a life on the road.

DAVID B. SCHREINER

ACTS 13:1–3; 14:26–28

PAUL'S GATEWAY TO THE WEST

According to Acts 13:1–3, Paul's first missionary journey began from the city of Antioch in Syria, roughly 425 miles north of Jerusalem. Although Luke provides little information about the church at Antioch, it appears to have served as a sort of home base for Paul. He spent time there before each of his three westward journeys.

Antioch was on the Orontes River, near present-day Antakya, Turkey. The city was built around 300 BC by Seleucus I, one of Alexander the Great's generals. As a strategic juncture between the Mediterranean coast and the mainland interior, Antioch quickly developed into a center of commerce, culture, and politics. During the Roman period it became the most important city in the empire after Rome and Alexandria, and it was a staging point for the Roman army.

Jews were present in Antioch from its earliest stages, and they might have been given Roman citizenship. Throughout the city's history, Jews were at the center of several violent encounters.[1] The presence of Jewish people in Antioch allowed the early Christians to rely on familiar social networks for the spread of the gospel. Yet Antioch's significance goes beyond the city's Jewish community. Rodney Stark has argued that urban centers with a certain profile—easy accessibility, ethnic diversity, and an openness to innovative ideas—became critical to the spread of Christianity.[2] Antioch certainly fit that bill. Its strategic position offered geographic opportunities that Jerusalem lacked, and its cosmopolitan and diverse character allowed Christianity to take root and spread quickly.

Antioch doesn't appear much in the New Testament, but its standing is evident. First, Antioch became an important staging area for the spread of the gospel, a place where missionaries regrouped.[3] In other words, it became the hub of early Christianity.

Antioch also uniquely experienced the question of how to include gentiles in the church. Acts 11:19–20 informs us that Antioch received the gospel soon after Steven was martyred. According to the text, some were "proclaiming the message to no one except Jews alone," while others "began to speak to the Hellenists also."[4] With this comment, Luke may be hinting at the controversies that would develop among the believers at Antioch. Eventually, this became the place where the question of gentile inclusion was hashed out with great passion, particularly among Paul and Peter (Galatians 2:11–14). Thus, the description of Antioch as the "crucible" for the development of Christianity seems correct.[5]

Finally, Antioch was the place where the label "Christian" was first used (Acts 11:26). It's fitting that the place responsible for staging Christianity's earliest missionary journeys also was the community that gave the young faith its name.

ANCIENT ROAD TO ANTIOCH

Paul launched his three westward journeys from this city in Syria.

THOMAS W. DAVIS

ACTS 13:4–12

A TURNING POINT IN THE APOSTOLIC MISSION

"The two of them, sent on their way by the Holy Spirit, went down [from Antioch] to Seleucia and from there sailed to Cyprus" (Acts 13:4 NIV). So the Acts of the Apostles records the beginning of the most important missionary trip in the history of the Christian church. The two missionaries, Paul and Barnabas, were joined by John Mark, the cousin of Barnabas, who was to serve as their assistant.

The first target of the mission trip is Cyprus, the third-largest island in the Mediterranean Sea. After Caesar Augustus gained solitary power in the Roman Empire, he made Cyprus a senatorial province, governed by a proconsul. By the beginning of the first century AD, Cyprus was already becoming a political backwater in the Roman Empire.

It is probably Barnabas who persuaded the Antioch church that Cyprus should be the first "foreign" mission field for the fledgling congregation. Perhaps it was a way for the Antioch believers to partially repay the debt they owed to their "spiritual midwives" from Cyprus who had brought them into the new faith. It also was a safe choice, since some of the congregation probably had family ties and commercial links to the island. The Cypriot city of Salamis, Barnabas' hometown, was only a day's sail from the port of Antioch at Seleucia. Pottery and coins from Antioch recovered in excavations on Cyprus document the strong commercial ties between the city and the island.

FROM SALAMIS TO PAPHOS

Salamis, where the mission team landed, contained all the urban amenities characteristic of a successful and prosperous eastern Roman city. Travelers entering the city from the harbor would pass through a major bath/gymnasium complex graced with fine statuary and elegant frescoes. Paul and Barnabas then would have encountered a magnificent theater with a seating capacity of 15,000. An estimate based on the city's aqueduct capacity suggests roughly 120,000 people lived at Salamis in the first century. All of this would have been familiar and comfortable territory for Paul.

Historical sources show that Salamis had a very large community of Jews, who were encouraged to settle there before Roman rule. Acts 13:5 supports the scenario of a large Jewish population when it reports that Paul and Barnabas proclaimed their message in the "Jewish synagogues"—plural, not singular.

SERGIUS PAULUS' NAME INSCRIBED
An inscription bearing the Cypriot governor's name was discovered at his hometown of Pisidian Antioch, where Paul and Barnabas traveled soon after visiting him on Cyprus.

The missionaries' journey across the island ends at Paphos, the capital of the Roman province of Cyprus. Paphos had been severely damaged in an earthquake, prompting Augustus to intervene and help repair the city. The Roman style-city Paul entered is hard to envision, and its remains are almost completely obscured by the monumental public buildings and magnificent urban villas of the second and third centuries AD. The city was graced with an excellent harbor that supported trade. The main civic theater, recently uncovered by archaeologists, could hold 8,500 people.

An examination of recent scholarship on Roman Cyprus suggests that the province was not as unified in the first century as previously thought. The elite of Paphos appear to have embraced elements of a separate cultural identity from the rest of Cyprus. New archaeological studies indicate an east/west economic divide in Roman Cyprus between Paphos and the eastern two-thirds of the island. Paphos appears to be a particularly "Roman" district. This may explain why, in the Acts narrative, Luke shifts the sequence of naming the apostles. Before this point Barnabas had priority, but from here on out Paul will be listed first. Barnabas is at home in Jerusalem, Antioch, and eastern Cyprus, but when the story shifts to Roman-oriented Paphos he is out of his depth, and Paul becomes the spokesman and leader because he embraces the cultural challenge.

A PIVOTAL DINNER PARTY

It seems likely that Paul and Barnabas were invited to be part of the after-dinner "entertainment" at a banquet given by the Roman governor, Sergius Paulus. Philosophical readings and discussions would have been a normal part of the evening at the home of an "intelligent man"—that is, one who was educated and interested in philosophical questions and therefore open to a new faith. The inclusion of the Jewish magician Bar-Jesus makes it almost a certainty that this was more of a social occasion than an official meeting held during office hours.

A recent study of Roman Cypriot magic texts makes clear that Luke's account of the contest between Bar-Jesus and Paul accurately reflects a Cypriot social setting. According to these texts, magic was often employed to prevent someone from speaking, and blindness could be used as a preventative measure in these cases. In Acts 13, Bar-Jesus is trying to prevent Paul from speaking to the governor about the Christian faith, so in typical Lukan irony the magician is struck down by the very weapon he was probably trying to use against Paul. The governor, on the other hand, speaks with Paul and is converted to faith.

The governor's conversion probably changed the itinerary of the mission, since he was from Pisidian Antioch in Galatia. Although Paul and Barnabas sail

ANCIENT PAPHOS

View from the governor's residence.

from Paphos to Perga, a major city on the mainland of Asia Minor, recent studies indicate that this voyage was not a normal route in the first century. A more typical trade route from Paphos would have taken the apostles south to Egypt. Under this scenario, they seem to have changed their plans to fulfill the governor's wishes to take the gospel to his family and hometown in Galatia.

It is now reasonable to propose that, in Paphos, Paul left behind the economic, social, and religious comfort zone in which he had spent his entire Christian ministry. Therefore, when Paul met the governor, it is certainly possible that he was for the first time forced to confront new possibilities in his Christian mission. The positive results of his encounter with the governor—in contrast to the apparent failure of the synagogue mission in Salamis, within Paul's comfort zone—may provide the catalyst for a fundamental change in Paul's ministry: he came to embrace the truly pagan world as his mission field. Luke underlines the profound importance of this shift by henceforth referring to the apostle using his Roman name, Paul, as opposed to his Jewish name, Saul.

Consequently, when Paul returns to Antioch after the journey to Cyprus and Galatia, he has been transformed, the gospel message has been transformed, and as a result the "Followers of the Way" will be transformed. "On arriving there, they gathered the church together and reported all that God had done through them and how he had opened a door of faith to the Gentiles" (Acts 14:27 NIV). The invitation to Jews to accept the Messiah of God had become an open door to the entire pagan world, and a Jewish messianic sect would become the Christian church. The crucible for all these changes is Cyprus.

ON CYPRUS, PAUL CAME TO EMBRACE THE TRULY PAGAN WORLD AS HIS MISSION FIELD.

PAUL AND BARNABAS AT PAPHOS

At the Kykkos Monastery on Cyprus, this fresco depicts the missionaries' encounter with Bar-Jesus and Sergius Paulus.

JOHN D. BARRY

ACTS 13:4–12

THE GOSPEL ADVANCES WITH POWER

Acts 13:4–12 records one of the most bizarre scenes in the New Testament. But it's also one of the most profound.

It's AD 46. The church at Antioch has just commissioned Paul and Barnabas as missionaries. Their first stop is the Mediterranean island of Cyprus, where Barnabas grew up. With Barnabas' cousin, John Mark, they begin proclaiming the message of Jesus to the local Jewish population of Salamis, a commercial hub of Cyprus. From there, they spread the good news about Jesus' death and resurrection across the island. They eventually reach Paphos, the political center of Cyprus and a major port city. And that's when things get very crazy, very fast.

In Paphos, they meet "a certain magician, a Jewish false prophet named Bar-Jesus" (Acts 13:6 ESV). This magician seems to have the ear of the local Roman governor, Sergius Paulus. His intent: to turn the governor against the gospel and thus against Paul, Barnabas, and Mark. The reason is probably power and money. If Sergius Paulus receives the gospel—and its power—he will no longer need the services of Bar-Jesus, and neither will the local population.

This is certainly the fear held by the owners of a demon-possessed slave-girl whom Paul later frees in Philippi (Acts 16). And it appears to have been the fear of

THE HOLY SPIRIT IS OVERCOMING PHYSICAL AND SPIRITUAL RESISTANCE TO BRING JESUS' SAVING MESSAGE **EVERYWHERE.**

Simon the Magician, who tries to buy the power of the Holy Spirit (Acts 8). And this is profound lesson number one from the mission to Cyprus in Acts 13: money and power are often the reasons why people oppose the gospel.

Paul doesn't tolerate the nonsense. He looks right at Bar-Jesus and tells him he is hindering the ways of the Lord. God is making a path straight and this man is doing the bidding of the devil. Paul then says: "Behold, the hand of the Lord is upon you, and you will be blind and unable to see the sun for a time" (Acts 13:11 ESV). And suddenly Bar-Jesus is blinded, searching in the darkness. Just like Paul was once temporarily blind (Acts 9:8), he makes Bar-Jesus blind. Paul once had to be led around by the hand, and now Bar-Jesus will be.

Paul is the embodiment of the song *Amazing Grace:* "I once was blind but now I see." He had once persecuted the church, but after hearing Jesus' voice he saw the truth. Paul brings the same gift to Bar-Jesus—he gives him the opportunity to be blind so that he may come to see again. This is profound lesson number two: sometimes people must experience the darkness of blindness before they can see the light.

But the lesson is not for Bar-Jesus alone. The Roman governor, Sergius Paulus, comes to Jesus in this moment. Astonished at the teachings of Jesus—which he has just witnessed in practice through an act of the Holy Spirit—Sergius Paulus chooses to believe. The Holy Spirit has shown power over both the spiritual and physical realm. A member of the devil's spiritual realm has been defeated. And now a member of the Roman government, representing the physical powers of the world, has come to Christ. This is profound lesson number three: the Holy Spirit is greater than any force, seen or unseen.

There is also a grand and wonderful message rooted in the overall narrative of Acts. This story represents the beginning of the endgame of the church—to bring the message of salvation in Jesus to all the earth. Luke, the author of Acts, is showing us that while the gospel may have begun with Jewish people worshiping a Jewish Messiah, it's now beginning to reach beyond people of Jewish descent. The gospel is advancing into the confines of the most well-established systems in the non-Jewish world—the Roman government.

The efforts of Paul on Cyprus represent the Holy Spirit's work in full force. As the very presence of God on earth, the Holy Spirit is on the move. It is overcoming physical and spiritual resistance to bring Jesus' saving message everywhere. This same gospel is on the move today—and the need is still desperate, as there are still hundreds of millions of people yet to hear the name of Jesus. Like the earliest missionaries, we are called to bring Jesus' message to them, in the power of the Holy Spirit.

SAINT PAUL'S COLUMN IN PAPHOS

According to local tradition, Paul was tortured here when he brought the gospel to the island of Cyprus.

DAMASCUS

ANTIOCH

CYPRUS

PAPHOS

PISIDIAN ANTIOCH

STEPHEN WITMER

ACTS 13:13–52

THE GOOD NEWS OF SALVATION

The apostle Paul's sermon in Pisidian Antioch (Acts 13:14–43) is an important one—not least because it is our earliest sermon of Paul's that has been preserved with any substantial degree of detail. Even though it was delivered before Paul composed his New Testament letters, the sermon already hints at three themes we encounter in his later writings.

1

Paul locates the gospel within salvation history and the Hebrew scriptures. He begins by recounting God's redemptive work for Israel, starting with the patriarchs and continuing through Egypt, the exodus, the wilderness wandering, the conquest of Canaan, the period of the judges, the monarchy, and John the Baptist's ministry. Paul also emphasizes that Jesus is a descendant of David, a connection he writes about in Romans 1:3. Further, Paul asserts that Jesus' death fulfills the words of the Old Testament prophets and that multiple Hebrew scriptures refer directly to Jesus and his resurrection.

2

Paul stresses that salvation comes through the cross of Christ. His main goal in this sermon isn't to teach an ethical system. Rather, he announces that "to us has been sent the message of this salvation" and that "through [Jesus] forgiveness of sins is proclaimed to you" (Acts 13:26, 38).[1] This good news about salvation is grounded in specific historical events—Jesus' death and resurrection. This strong focus on the cross and the empty tomb remained central to Paul's teaching in the letters he wrote later in his ministry.[2]

3

Paul contrasts Christ and the law as pathways to salvation: "by [Jesus] everyone who believes is freed from everything from which you could not be freed by the law of Moses" (Acts 13:39). This sentence of the sermon brings together several Greek terms that characterize the theology of Paul's letters:

GREEK	ENGLISH
πιστεύω, *pisteuō*	to believe, to trust, to have faith
δικαιόω, *dikaioō*	to justify, to declare righteous (ESV: to free)
νόμος, *nomos*	law

The contrast between Christ and the law in this sermon foreshadows a major theological concept Paul writes about later. For example, in Galatians he affirms that "a person is not justified by works of the law but through faith in Jesus Christ" (Galatians 2:16).

These clear connections to Paul's letters give us insight into Acts 13 and suggest that this sermon, as recorded by Luke, is a faithful representation of Paul's actual preaching. The core content of Paul's gospel was already firmly established from the beginning of his ministry. After all, it was revealed to him directly by Jesus Christ (see Galatians 1:11–24).

In addition, the events that take place the following Sabbath—when Paul and Barnabas turn from the Jews to the gentiles and are driven out of the district—show that, early on, Paul established a strategy of beginning his evangelism efforts in a city's synagogue and turning to the gentiles after Jewish rejection.

Ultimately, the sermon at Pisidian Antioch shows us that, even in the beginning of his ministry, Paul's announcement of salvation was rooted firmly in the Hebrew scriptures and their culmination in Christ.

PISIDIAN ANTIOCH

The city where Paul preached his first recorded sermon.

JOSEPH R. DODSON

ACTS 14:8–20

A VISIT FROM THE GODS?

Several years ago, I lectured at the Károli Gáspár University in Budapest, Hungary. While I was there, my host took me hiking up to the Citadella on Gellért Hill. The Citadella affords a spectacular view of the city underlined by the Danube River. As we descended from the peak, I noticed a church carved into the rock at the base of the hill. At first I did not think much about it, but then my host told me the story behind the church at Gellért Hill.

"You see," he said, "the Citadella was the place where the first missionary to Hungary was dragged to the precipice, placed in a barrel, and cast down to his death." The pagans may have killed the missionary, but they did not stop the mission. In spite of the grisly death, other missionaries put their lives on the line and came to the city to share the love of Christ. As a result, eventually a church was established where that missionary had been martyred.

Knowing this tidbit of historical information helped me see Budapest and the gospel in a whole new light. Now the hill was much more than a photo opportunity for an Instagram post; it stood as a profound example of the ironic power of the

> GOD SENT PAUL AND BARNABAS NOT TO FLOOD THE PAGANS IN DIVINE WRATH, BUT TO INUNDATE THEM WITH THE LOVE OF CHRIST AND THE HOPE OF THE GOSPEL.

gospel. The gates of hell will never prevail against the church the Lord promised to establish upon the rock.

STORIES BEHIND THE STORY

Likewise, knowing the history behind the places Paul visited on his missionary journeys can help us understand and appreciate the narratives in radical new ways. When Luke wrote Acts (as a good ancient historian) he made allusions to the stories behind the stories. Allusions were often used to provide entertainment value.[1] To borrow from Benjamin Sommer, "allusions, like jokes, place familiar material in new, often surprising contexts."[2] The more I study Acts, the more I think there are a number of cases where Luke uses an allusion to be whimsical if not ironic.

For instance, you may recall that when Paul visits Athens, he quotes a Greek poet: "In him we live and move and have our being ... for we too are his offspring" (Acts 17:28).[3] In noting this, Luke demonstrates how Paul cleverly turns the pagans' own literature on its head in order to share the gospel of Jesus Christ. Also in Acts 17, Luke alludes to the story of Socrates, who—like Paul—stood on trial in Athens. It's as if Luke is winking at his audience, who would know that Socrates was charged with persuading people to acknowledge new gods, and now Paul was being accused of advocating foreign ones.[4] In addition to a number of other parallels to the famous trial of Socrates, Paul even begins his speech with the same words that Socrates used to start his defense: "Men, Athenians."[5]

Knowing the story behind the story, Luke's original audience may have been filled with suspense. Will Paul face the same mortal fate as Socrates? In an amusing twist, Luke demonstrates that although the great philosopher Socrates was incapable of talking his way out of a death sentence, Paul the "uneducated babbler" not only escapes execution but even converts some distinguished members of the audience.[6]

INTERPRETIVE INSIGHTS

Familiarity with this Greco-Roman background leads to a better understanding of Paul's evangelism strategy and the simple effectiveness of the gospel. Sometimes it also helps us understand why Paul's pagan audience responds to him the way they do. For example, in Acts 14, Paul peers into the eyes of a man who had been crippled from birth. Seeing that the man has enough faith to be healed, the apostle commands him to rise in the name of Christ—and he does! But in an incredible turn, the people of Lystra bow down and begin to worship Paul and Barnabas, thinking they must be Hermes and Zeus.

Even while the apostles are trying to convince the crowds they are ordinary men, a priest quickly brings an ox from Zeus' temple to slaughter in their honor, assuming they are gods come down from heaven. Why in the world would the Lystrians jump to such an extreme conclusion?

Knowing the story behind the story helps us appreciate what Luke and the original audience of Acts would have noticed and possibly considered comical. You see, just as the Jews were very familiar with the story of Noah's flood, so the Lystrians would have known a famous pagan myth about a different flood. In one version of the story, Zeus and Hermes become bored on top of Mount Olympus.[7]

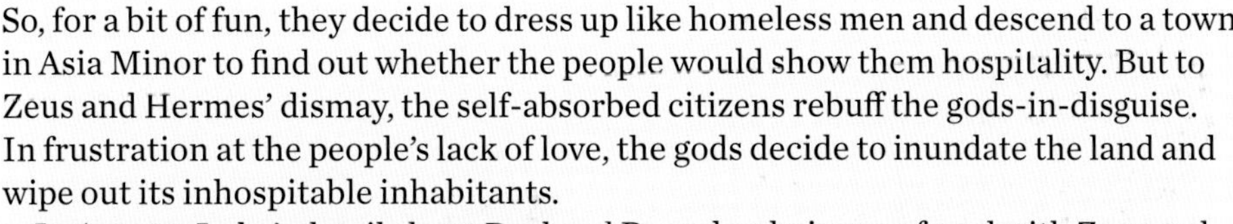

So, for a bit of fun, they decide to dress up like homeless men and descend to a town in Asia Minor to find out whether the people would show them hospitality. But to Zeus and Hermes' dismay, the self-absorbed citizens rebuff the gods-in-disguise. In frustration at the people's lack of love, the gods decide to inundate the land and wipe out its inhospitable inhabitants.

In Acts 14, Luke's detail about Paul and Barnabas being confused with Zeus and Hermes alludes to the story behind the story. When the ragtag apostle duo come to town as strangers and heal the paralytic, the people deduce that Hermes and Zeus are back at it again—and the Lystrians are dead set on *not* repeating their

THE CHURCH AT GELLÉRT HILL

This church in Budapest was established where the first missionary to Hungary was martyred.

cataclysmic mistake of failing to entertain the incognito gods. Luke likely intends to show that the Lystrians' extravagant reaction is driven by dread and superstition rather than piety and love. What the Lystrians do not understand, though, is that the One True God sent Paul and Barnabas *not* to flood the pagans in divine wrath, but to inundate them with the love of Christ and the hope of the gospel.

Eventually the pagans swing from worshiping Paul to stoning him and leaving him for dead. But like the old Hungarians, the Lystrians learned an indubitable truth: try as they might, they could not turn the tide of the gospel. Paul would get back up, Christ would be proclaimed, and the church would be established in their city (Acts 14:19–20). In fact, the church in Lystra would even go on to produce its own prominent missionary—Paul's son in the faith, Timothy (Acts 16:1–5).

PREACHING TO EVERYONE, EVERYWHERE

ECKHARD J. SCHNABEL

When Jesus called Paul to be his envoy—coinciding with Paul's conversion on the road to Damascus—he described two main elements to the new apostle's task:

1. Verbal proclamation: Paul shall share the good news of Jesus, Israel's Messiah and Savior of the world, through whom God grants forgiveness of sins and integration into God's messianic people; and

2. Unlimited geographical and social scope: Paul shall preach to gentiles and to the Jewish people, to ordinary people and to kings (Acts 9:15; 22:15; 26:16–18).

Assuming the plausibility of AD 30 as the year of Jesus' death and resurrection, Paul probably was converted to faith in Jesus Messiah in AD 31 or 32. Luke reports that Paul began his missionary work right away, in the city of Damascus, preaching in the synagogues that Jesus is the Son of God. We learn from Galatians 1:15 (read in light of 2 Corinthians 11:32) that Paul engaged in missionary work in Arabia/Nabatea, presumably preaching both to Jews in the synagogue communities as well as to gentiles. Then Paul was involved in the missionary work of the Jerusalem church; he preached fearlessly in the name of Jesus to the Greek-speaking Jews of the city.

When Paul's life became endangered, he moved to Tarsus—his hometown, the capital of the province of Cilicia—where he preached the faith he once tried to destroy. Paul's mission in Syria and Cilicia lasted eight or nine years (AD 34–42). Then Paul was active in Antioch, the capital of the Roman province of Syria. He was invited to Anitoch by Barnabas, who had asked him to come because "a great number of people" in the city were being converted (Acts 11:24).[1]

All of this means that the so-called "first missionary journey" (Acts 13–14) was in reality not Paul's first "journey" but rather the sixth, seventh, and eighth phases of his missionary work, beginning in AD 45 (see chart on page 48).

PAUL'S STRATEGY AND METHODS

The missionary strategy of the apostle Paul can be described as winning as many Jews and gentiles as possible for faith in Jesus as Israel's Messiah and Savior of the world (1 Corinthians 9:19). The principal methods that Paul used to implement this strategy follow logically: he preached the gospel to Jews in synagogues, and he preached the gospel to gentiles or polytheists, whom he found in synagogues, in the agora (the central plaza of a city), and in private houses.[2]

Paul evidently traveled to geographically adjacent regions, provinces, and cities where people were open to listen to his message. When he was driven out of a city, he left.[3] When new opportunities arose, he used them (for example, see below regarding the mission in Pisidian Antioch).

When we read the description of Paul's missionary work in the book of Acts, we need to remember that the author, Luke, is reporting selectively. He does not mention all of Paul's activities in a particular city or all the events that transpired. Sometimes Luke focuses on the preaching in synagogues. Acts 13:16–41, set in Pisidian Antioch, records a long sermon that is not repeated in the reports of Paul's missionary work in other cities. However, the opposition of Jews from Antioch and Iconium who came to Lystra implies that Paul preached before the Jews in Lystra, which Luke does not explicitly report. Likewise, Luke sometimes focuses on a particular miracle and its impact on the gentile population (such as in Acts 14:8–18).

The fact that Paul's activities in Derbe and Perge are reported in merely a few words does not mean that nothing much happened in those cities.[4] Readers can assume that Paul preached in the synagogues of Derbe and Perge the same kind of sermon reported for Pisidian Antioch in Acts 13:16–41. They also can assume that miracles happened similar to those in Lystra, and that the new converts were disciples "filled with joy and with the Holy Spirit" just as they were in Antioch (Acts 13:52). Luke notes that Paul and Barnabas had to leave Iconium in a hurry because they heard that people wanted to stone them. Then he reports that the apostles went to Lystra and Derbe "and to the surrounding country" (Acts 14:6)—which indicates they preached in the smaller towns and villages controlled by Lystra and Derbe, even though Luke doesn't report what happened there.

Paul uses any opportunity to preach the gospel that presents itself. In Acts 13:13–14, the narrative shifts from the city of Paphos (on the island of Cyprus) to Perge on the mainland coast and then to Pisidian Antioch, an inland city of Galatia. Perge, the capital of the province of Pamphylia, had perhaps 75,000 inhabitants, and there were other large towns in the region. The apostles' decision to leave this major population center and travel north to Pisidian Antioch, with a mere 10,000 people, can hardly be explained as a "strategic" move. It has been suggested—on the basis of Paul's reference to a "physical infirmity" in Galatians 4:13—that he went to Pisidian Antioch because he had contracted malaria and sought relief in the higher altitudes (Pisidian Antioch was in the Anatolian highlands).

Another (and perhaps more plausible) explanation involves Sergius Paulus, the governor of Cyprus who was converted in Paphos. He belonged to the family of the Sergii Paulli, who owned estates in Galatia. Ancient inscriptions confirm

PAUL USES ANY OPPORTUNITY TO PREACH THE GOSPEL THAT PRESENTS ITSELF.

16 PHASES OF PAUL'S MINISTRY

Although Paul's missionary work is traditionally divided into three journeys, that approach overlooks the previous 14 years of his ministry, as well as his activity toward the end of his life. New Testament professor Eckhard Schnabel recommends a 16-phase framework based on the Roman provinces and cities where Paul preached.

Phase	Location	Year (AD)	Supporting texts
1	Damascus	32/33	Acts 9:19–21, 23-25; Galatians 1:17
2	Arabia/Nabatea	32–33	Galatians 1:17; 2 Corinthians 11:32
3	Jerusalem	33/34	Acts 9:26–29; Romans 1:16
4	Syria/Cilicia; Tarsus	34–42	Acts 9:30; 11:25–26; Galatians 1:21
5	Syria: Antioch	42–44	Acts 11:26–30; 13:1
6	Cyprus: Salamis, Paphos	45	Acts 13:4–12
7	Galatia: Pisidian Antioch, Iconium, Lystra, Derbe	45–47	Acts 13:14–14:23
8	Pamphylia: Perge	47	Acts 14:24–26
9	Macedonia: Philippi, Thessalonica, Berea	49–50	Acts 16:6–17:15
10	Achaia: Athens, Corinth	50–51	Acts 17:16–18:28
11	Asia: Ephesus	52–55	Acts 19:1–41
12	Illyricum	56	Romans 15:19
13	Judea, Caesarea	57–59	Acts 21:27–26:32
14	Rome	60–62	Acts 28:17–28
15	Spain	63–64 ?	1 Clement 5:5–7 *
16	Crete	64–65 ?	Titus 1:5

*First Clement is a letter from the church of Rome to the church of Corinth that has been dated to the end of the first century (AD 95–96). The text indicates that Paul preached the gospel "to the extremity of the West" (i.e., Spain).

that members of this family lived in Pisidian Antioch. Classical scholar Stephen Mitchell thinks it highly plausible that the governor of Cyprus suggested that Paul spend time in Pisidian Antioch and gave him letters of introduction to the governor's family, to aid the apostles' passage and stay in the city.[5]

PREACHING TO ALL PEOPLES

When we survey the people with whom Paul and Barnabas had contact during their mission in the provinces of Cyprus, Galatia, and Pamphylia, we see the unlimited ethnic and social scope of their missionary work:

- They preached the gospel in cities (Salamis, Paphos, Antioch, Iconium, Lystra, Derbe, Perge). They also preached in small towns and villages in the countryside controlled by the larger cities.
- They preached the gospel before Jewish audiences in Salamis, Paphos, Antioch, Iconium, and presumably in Lystra and Derbe.
- They preached before proselytes, gentiles who had converted to Judaism.
- They preached to "Godfearers" (Acts 13:16, 26)—gentiles who were impressed by the Jewish religion and attended synagogue services.
- They preached before gentile "women of high standing" (Acts 13:50) who might not have regularly attended synagogue services but who sympathized with the Jewish faith.
- They preached before gentiles—pagan sympathizers with the Jewish God and polytheists who worshiped other deities, such as Zeus and Hermes.
- They had contact with members of the local Jewish elite, the officials of the synagogue.
- They had contact with the "leading men of the city" (13:50)—the members of the local elite who constituted the municipal aristocracy, people who controlled the public life in the city due to their social standing and wealth from their estates.
- They preached before Jews who still might have spoken Hebrew and/or Aramaic; they preached in Greek before gentile audiences; and they preached before people whose mother language was Lycaonian.
- They preached to the general population—people who were mostly poor, like the crippled beggar in Lystra who presumably sat in the agora.
- They had contact with people who practiced magic.
- They had contact with—and converted—a Roman governor, Sergius Paulus, who controlled the empire's province of Cyprus.

Paul preaches to any and all people, wherever he can find them. When he is forced out of a city, he preaches in the neighboring region. There are always more people who need to hear the gospel. This is why Paul does not stop preaching—because, as he says, "I am compelled to preach. Woe to me if I do not preach the gospel!" (1 Corinthians 9:16).

THERE ARE ALWAYS MORE PEOPLE WHO NEED TO HEAR THE GOSPEL. THIS IS WHY PAUL DOES NOT STOP PREACHING.

TIMOTHY GOMBIS

THE GOOD NEWS CROSSES ETHNIC BORDERS

The time Paul spent in the church in Antioch (in Syria), along with his experiences during his first mission with Barnabas, shaped his conception of the gospel. And the controversy that led to the first church council in Jerusalem, along with the trouble the churches in Galatia faced, sharpened Paul's arguments regarding the place of the gentiles among the people of God.

In the mid-30s AD, several years after his conversion, Paul made his first visit to Jerusalem as a disciple of Jesus. Because that resulted in some Jews plotting to kill him, the church sent him to his hometown of Tarsus, where he spent the next eight years. During that time, a multiethnic church made up of Jews and gentiles was founded in Antioch, and the Jerusalem church sent Barnabas there to look after that community.

Around AD 44, Barnabas sent for Paul to come from Tarsus to join him in ministering to the church at Antioch. Paul's participation in a church made up of Jewish and non-Jewish Jesus-followers must have powerfully shaped his conception of the gospel as the means by which God was restoring the unity of humanity in Christ. More than simply a theological conception, living in community and sharing meals together would have made this gospel truth a living reality.

UNITY IN GALATIA

Not long after Paul had joined Barnabas in Antioch, the Spirit of God called the church to send Barnabas and Paul on a mission. During this mission to Cyprus and Galatia, the apostles first visited synagogues wherever they went, preaching the gospel of Jesus Christ as the climax and fulfillment of Israel's scriptures. Reaction by those in the synagogues was mixed, with some Jews responding positively to Barnabas and Paul and others rejecting their message.

After facing trouble in several places, the missionaries declared that they were going to the gentiles, since this was their calling. A group of Jews—some who had previously objected to Barnabas and Paul in Antioch and Iconium—exploited the unrest in Lystra to turn the crowd against Paul, who was then dragged outside the city and stoned. After recovering miraculously, Paul continued on the mission, and the apostles arrived next in Derbe.

The Galatian churches were founded around this time. In Galatians 4:13–14, Paul reminds these new Christians that it was because of a bodily condition that he had the occasion to preach the gospel to them initially, and he notes that his appearance was "a trial" to them. He has in mind how awful he looked after being crushed under heavy stones thrown or dropped on him by the angry mob at Lystra. Rather than rejecting Paul, the Galatians treated him as an angel of God and even as Christ himself, he writes. These gentiles showed Paul wonderful hospitality, and small communities of Jesus-followers were formed in response to the mission team's preaching of the gospel.

Paul's training as a Pharisee—a Jewish group that was passionate for the purity of God's people and for Israel's faithfulness to Torah—would have nurtured in him an attitude of exclusion toward non-Jews among the people of God. But his commission by the exalted Lord Jesus, his experience in a multiethnic church, and the response among the gentiles during his first mission would have shaped Paul's theology and practice of radical ethnic inclusion among God's people.

CONFLICT IN ANTIOCH

At some point after Paul and Barnabas returned to Antioch, Peter visited from Jerusalem and experienced the radical character of the gospel by sharing table fellowship with non-Jews—something he formerly thought was "unlawful."[1] However, when other Jews came to Antioch from the Jerusalem church—Jews whose commitment to the purity of Israel did not allow them to imagine that fellowship with gentiles was possible—Peter was intimidated, along with some of the other Jewish Christians, and they refused to eat with the non-Jews. This caused tremendous confusion in the church, signaling to the gentiles that they were being shut out of the people of God.

We learn in Galatians 2:14 that Paul confronted Peter's "hypocrisy," since Peter really knew better. He had already discovered that God does not show favoritism based on ethnicity and that all who call on the name of the Lord will be saved (Acts 10:1–11:18). It makes no sense to fellowship with gentiles as gentiles and enjoy the freedom of living with others in God's inclusive family, only to pull back and require gentiles to become Jews in order to remain among God's people.

Paul proceeded to argue that because Jewish Christians have been crucified with Christ, they are already dead to the law and can be set free into the enjoyment of the relationships that were created through God's blessing of Abraham.[2]

WHAT MATTERS, ACCORDING TO PAUL, IS NOT JEWISH OR NON-JEWISH IDENTITY, BUT THE REALITY THAT THE NEW CREATION HAS ARRIVED.

This may have been the same incident that Luke records in Acts 15, where a similar group from the Jerusalem church arrived in Antioch to press the non-Jewish Christians to convert to Judaism for salvation. Because of the confusion this caused, the believers in Antioch commissioned Paul and Barnabas to go and meet with leaders of the Jerusalem church to decide the issue.

RESOLUTION IN JERUSALEM

At some point before arriving in Jerusalem, Paul received word that Jewish missionaries from the Jerusalem church were teaching the same thing in the churches in Galatia. Paul's passionate response is reflected in the fiery letter he writes to the Galatians, calling down curses on anyone causing disruption by teaching what he calls "another gospel."[3]

Paul notes that during a previous visit to Jerusalem he had brought Titus with him as a sort of "test case" for whether a gentile Christian was a full member of God's people. Even though pressure was brought to bear to have Titus circumcised, they resisted so that the purity of the gospel might remain—the reality that anyone of any ethnicity can call on God and receive salvation (Galatians 2:1–5).

At the end of his letter to the Galatians, Paul makes this affirmation: what matters is not Jewish or non-Jewish identity, but the reality that the new creation has arrived. In this era, the Spirit was being poured out on the church and was spilling over the ethnic boundaries that divided the Jewish and non-Jewish worlds.

After much debate, the Jerusalem leadership saw things in very similar terms. After hearing from Peter, whose experience confirmed that God was building one new multiethnic family, James gave the final ruling: gentiles should feel no pressure from Jewish Christians to convert to Judaism in order to enjoy salvation. The council meeting in Acts 15 ends with the writing of a letter to make the decision official.

The outcome of the Jerusalem Council paved the way for the rest of Paul's ministry. With the resolution of the gentile question—and the approval of James and other church leaders—Paul was free to pursue his mission with confidence.

Paul's calling to proclaim Christ to the gentiles did not mean he was abandoning his ancestral faith in the God of Israel. On the contrary, Paul believed that the time had come when God was extending his salvation to the entire world, fulfilling the ultimate vision of the scriptures.

- *God's promise to Abraham:* "All the nations of the earth shall gain blessing for themselves through your offspring" (Genesis 26:4).[4]

- *The prophecy of Isaiah:* "In days to come the mountain of the Lord's house shall be established as the highest of the mountains, and shall be raised above the hills; all the nations shall stream to it" (Isaiah 2:2).

The catalyst for the gentiles' inclusion, Paul believed, was Jesus' death and resurrection: through the Messiah, the way had opened for the whole world to join God's family. This belief was confirmed by the outpouring of the Holy Spirit among gentile believers from Syria to Cyprus to Galatia.

As Acts 15 records, the church leaders in Jerusalem affirmed this new stage in God's plan. And with the blessing of the apostles, Paul committed himself to spreading the gospel in Asia Minor and beyond.

David Roberts, "Jerusalem from the South" (1839)

PAUL'S SECOND MISSIONARY JOURNEY

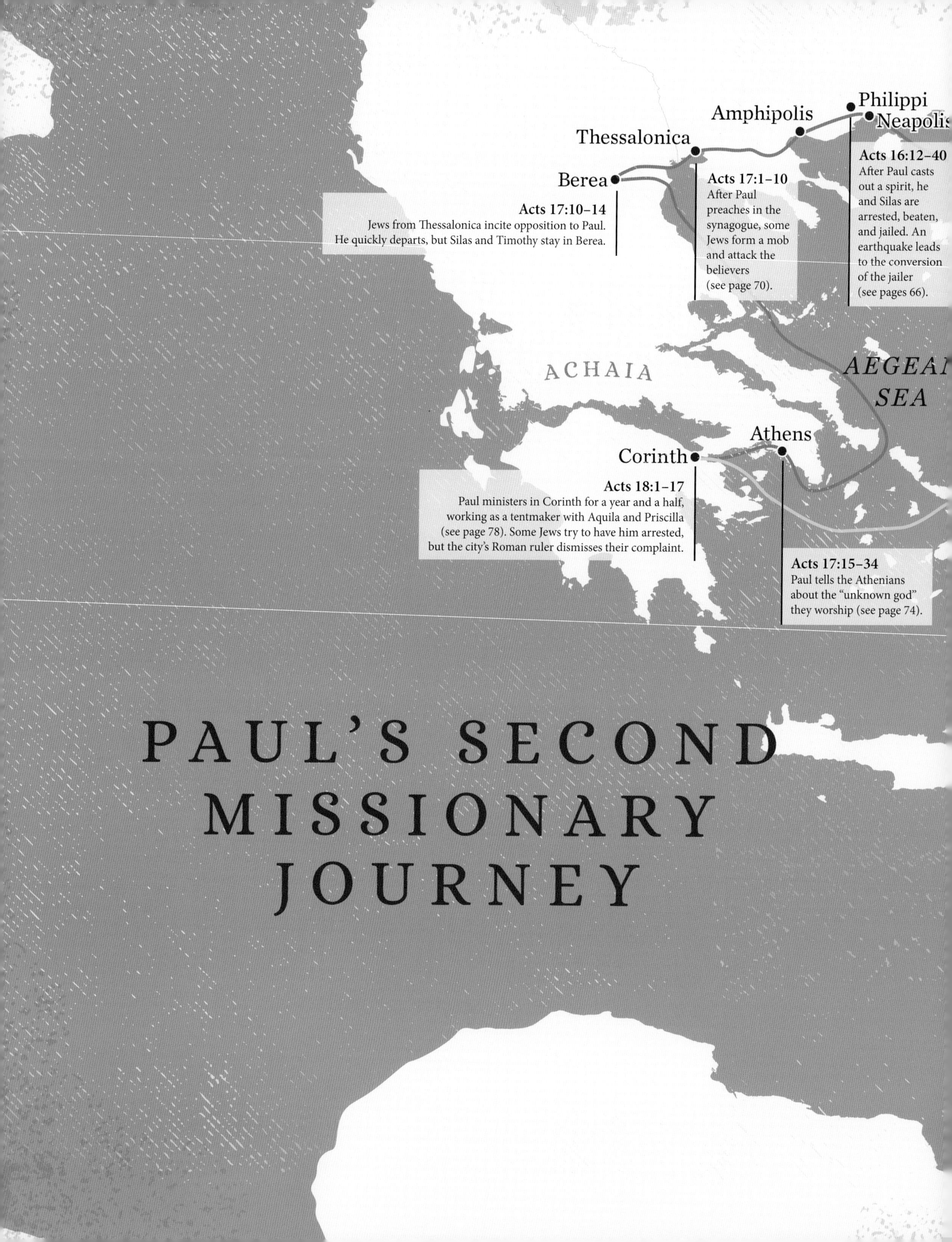

Philippi

Amphipolis

Neapolis

Thessalonica

Berea

Acts 16:12–40
After Paul casts out a spirit, he and Silas are arrested, beaten, and jailed. An earthquake leads to the conversion of the jailer (see pages 66).

Acts 17:1–10
After Paul preaches in the synagogue, some Jews form a mob and attack the believers (see page 70).

Acts 17:10–14
Jews from Thessalonica incite opposition to Paul. He quickly departs, but Silas and Timothy stay in Berea.

ACHAIA

AEGEA SEA

Athens

Corinth

Acts 18:1–17
Paul ministers in Corinth for a year and a half, working as a tentmaker with Aquila and Priscilla (see page 78). Some Jews try to have him arrested, but the city's Roman ruler dismisses their complaint.

Acts 17:15–34
Paul tells the Athenians about the "unknown god" they worship (see page 74).

churches from Paul's letters: the Philippians, the Thessalonians, the Corinthians.

Luke's account of the second mission begins in the city of Antioch, where Paul found a new ministry partner in Silas. Along with Timothy, the newly forged team was able to minister to several cities in Asia Minor.

Although Philippi was not part of Paul's original travel plan, he obeyed God's calling by bringing the gospel to the Macedonians. When he and Silas were thrown in jail under false accusations, the two men used their chains as an opportunity to preach the good news to the jailer.

After Paul's preaching in Thessalonica led to threatening opposition by some of the Jews there, he pressed on to Berea where he and Silas were warmly received. But when the opponents followed Paul to Berea, he was forced to move on again and separate from Silas and Timothy, his dear friends and partners in the gospel.

Quite unexpectedly, Paul found himself alone in Athens, yet he did not succumb to frustration or merely bide his time. Instead, he challenged the idolatry and philosophers of Athens by proclaiming the uniqueness of the God who raised Jesus from the dead. It's unclear whether Paul formed a church there, but his speech to the Athenians is a powerful legacy of Christian witness in the face of skepticism.

During his 18-month stay in Corinth, Paul labored patiently for the gospel amid strong opposition, both from Jews who rejected his message and from secular authorities.

Despite the initial setbacks, Paul continued to move forward in his calling as apostle to the gentiles by preaching the gospel no matter the location or the circumstances. He extended his evangelistic efforts into Europe for the first time, planted several new churches, and helped bring many people to saving faith in Jesus. Paul's ministry was based on his confidence in God's ability to spread the gospel regardless of any obstacles and opponents. This trust undoubtedly propelled Paul forward in his missionary efforts.

"View of Corinth," from History of Xerxes the Great *by Jacob Abbott (1900)*

THRACE
BLACK SEA
BITHYNIA
Acts 16:6–8
The Holy Spirit restrains the missionaries from preaching in Asia and Bithynia, so they press on to Troas.
Troas
MYSIA
ASIA
Acts 16:9–11
Paul's vision of a Macedonian man sends the team across the Aegean Sea (see page 62).
GALATIA
PHRYGIA
Ephesus
Acts 18:18–21
Aquila and Priscilla accompany the missionaries to Ephesus. Although the Jews show an interest in the gospel, Paul declines to stay in the city but pledges to return.
Iconium
Acts 16:1–5
Timothy joins the mission team.
Lystra
Derbe
PAMPHYLIA
LYCIA
CYPRUS
MEDITERRANEAN SEA

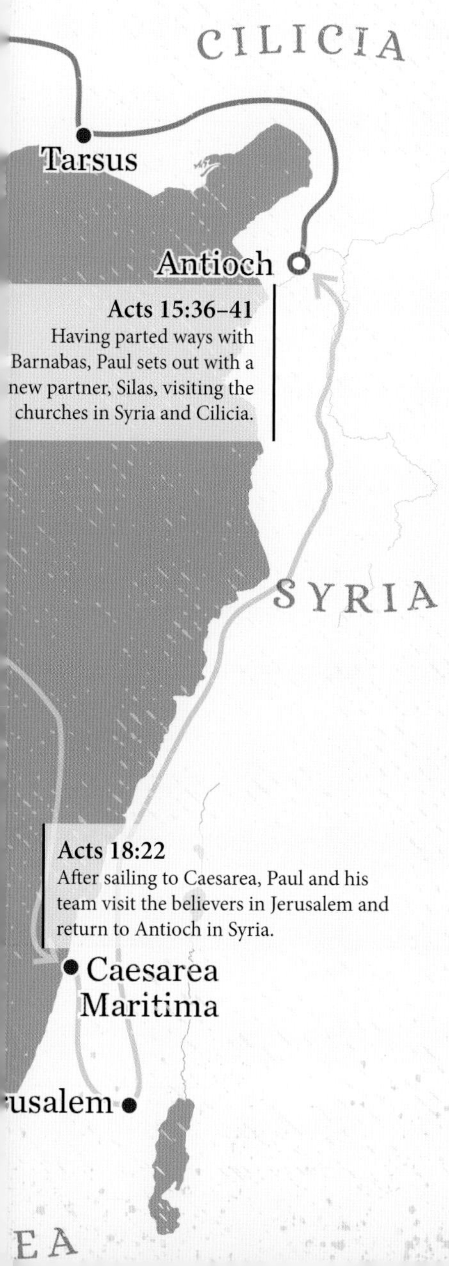

Paul's Travel Companions on the Second Missionary Journey

Silas

Acts doesn't mention Silas' background, but we can assume he was—like Paul—a Jew who became a follower of Jesus. In the account of the Jerusalem Council, Silas is introduced as a church leader and a prophet (Acts 15:22, 32). He is chosen by the apostles and elders to deliver the council's decision regarding gentiles to the churches in Syria and Cilicia (15:27).

In Antioch, Silas had an edifying ministry among the gentile believers—which likely contributed to Paul choosing him as a new missionary partner after Paul and Barnabas parted ways. Silas also ministered alongside Peter in Rome (1 Peter 5:12; the Greek text of Peter's and Paul's letters refer to him as "Silvanus").

Timothy

Timothy joined the mission team in his hometown of Lystra, one of the Galatian cities where Paul planted a church during the first missionary journey. Timothy came out of a mixed marriage, with a Jewish mother and a gentile father. This led to a complicated question regarding circumcision. Paul advocated freedom from the law for gentiles, and the Jerusalem Council had ruled that gentiles did not need to be circumcised (Acts 15). But what do you do with someone who's *both* gentile and Jewish?

Paul didn't want Timothy's dual ethnicity to become an issue in the way of the gospel, so he had Timothy circumcised as a Jew—and yet, because Timothy was also gentile, he could be effective at reaching out to non-Jews with the gospel.

Luke

According to church tradition, Luke wrote Acts as sequel to his Gospel. Many scholars believe Luke traveled with Paul and wrote portions of Acts as his eyewitness account. One often-cited piece of supporting evidence involves the "we" passages of Acts—where the narrator shifts from a third-person perspective (referring to the missionaries as "they") to a first-person perspective ("we").

The first "we" passage comes at Acts 16:10, as Paul and his team are preparing to sail from Troas to Macedonia. The use of "we" continues at Philippi (16:16), but then the narrator switches back to "they."

When the missionaries come back through Philippi on the third journey (20:5–6), the use of "we" and "us" resumes—and continues through the group's arrival at Jerusalem (21:18). Luke's report of Paul's sea voyage, shipwreck, and arrival at Rome (27:1–28:16) also use "we" and "us." The implication is that Luke was traveling with Paul ever since his final visit to Philippi (20:5–6).

Three of Paul's letters indicate that his travel companions included Luke (Colossians 4:14; 2 Timothy 4:11; Philemon 24). In Colossians 4:14, Paul identifies Luke as a doctor.

Compiled from Lexham Bible Dictionary and Logos Mobile Education

Acts 15:36–41
Having parted ways with Barnabas, Paul sets out with a new partner, Silas, visiting the churches in Syria and Cilicia.

Acts 18:22
After sailing to Caesarea, Paul and his team visit the believers in Jerusalem and return to Antioch in Syria.

THE SECOND
MISSIONARY JOURNEY

ACTS 15:36–18:22

THE UNSTOPPABLE GOSPEL

After the success of his first westward journey and the decision of the Jerusalem Council (Acts 13:1–15:35), Paul probably felt confident about his missionary work. He and Barnabas had preached the gospel to many people, and the Jerusalem church offered approval of his mission to the gentiles. By all appearances, Paul's evangelistic efforts seemed to be going in the right direction.

That confidence was likely crushed before Paul departed on a second mission. He and Barnabas had a major disagreement, ultimately resulting in the two evangelists going their separate ways. Despite winning support for his gentile mission, Paul was still working to repair the rift between Jews and gentiles in the Galatian churches. According to Acts 16, Paul apparently had no intention of traveling beyond Asia Minor.[1] There was every reason to have limited expectations.

The Holy Spirit had other ideas.

The mission that unfolded was a far-reaching success, launching Paul and his new team of coworkers across the Aegean Sea to Macedonia and Achaia where they planted new gospel communities, mainly among gentiles. We know some these

PAUL THE TRAVELER

A DAY'S JOURNEY WITH PAUL

CARYN A. REEDER

Paul, Silas, and Timothy covered quite a distance during the second missionary journey: roughly 880 miles from Antioch to Troas, 420 miles from Philippi to Corinth, and 468 miles from Jerusalem back to Antioch—plus another 1,190 miles across the sea. To cover just these distances (not counting the detours to visit churches along the way), the travelers would have walked for at least 90 days along local tracks, unpaved roads, and imperial highways, and sailed at least 11 days in merchant ships.[1] In all, the "journey" portion of Paul's second mission trip was a significant undertaking.

However, we do not hear much about the actual journey in Acts 15:36–18:22. The story moves quickly through Paul's travels, listing regions and cities one after another and giving a sense of urgency with words like "immediately."[2] But behind the fast-moving narrative are long days on the road, uncomfortable nights in inns, and the dangers of bandits, pirates, and storms at sea.

What would it have been like to be on the road with Paul? Working from travelers' stories, inscriptions, archaeological remains, and other sources, we can reconstruct the experience of a journey in the first century.[3]

ROAD WARRIORS

Travelers in the first century risked theft, diarrhea, kidnapping, and more. But despite these concerns, people regularly traveled throughout the Roman Empire. Governors, messengers, tax collectors, and others traveled on official business. Soldiers, their families, and their slaves were constantly on the move, patrolling the roads, marching to new postings, and carting supplies. Merchants and slave traders crossed the Empire with cloth, grain, pottery, and human lives. Other travelers were on the way to visit family or friends, study abroad, look for work, seek treatment for illnesses, and see the sights.

Like most travelers in the Roman Empire, Paul, Silas, and Timothy likely walked long distances, carrying their possessions in knapsacks. The average person could cover 18 to 20 miles in a day, depending on the weather and terrain. Along the major roads, walkers would hear merchant wagons and passenger carriages from miles away as their iron-shod wheels clanked over paving stones. By the middle of the day, they might have envied the very wealthy in their luxurious private carriages or litters carried by slaves. These travelers had a smooth enough ride to read books, write letters, and take naps.

On major roads, Paul, Silas, and Timothy would want to keep out of the way of the fastest travelers: officials and messengers on government business, riding on horseback between relay stations. They also would watch for Roman soldiers on patrol. The soldiers were there for public safety and security, but they were also known to demand bribes and abuse civilians. Above all, Paul and his companions had to be on guard against wild animals, thieves, and bandits (and, on the seas or along the coast, pirates). It was not uncommon for travelers to be kidnapped for ransom, sold into slavery, or murdered along the roads. Some travelers simply disappeared.

BEHIND THE FAST-MOVING NARRATIVE OF ACTS ARE LONG DAYS ON THE ROAD, UNCOMFORTABLE NIGHTS IN INNS, AND THE DANGERS OF BANDITS, PIRATES, AND STORMS AT SEA.

SAFETY AND SHELTER

Paul and his friends faced plenty of less exciting—but equally hazardous—hardships on their journey: bad weather, unsanitary food and water, and the annoyances of dust, mud, and insects. Travelers' stories record delays and illnesses due to extreme heat, storms, bad water from springs, and bad food from taverns. Even more mundane are the trials of blistered feet, tired legs, and boredom. Trudging along with Paul for a day would be exhausting, but he surely kept Silas and Timothy engaged and entertained with good conversation. It's easy to imagine the three missionaries debating the interpretation of Scripture and planning sermons or letters to their churches as they walked.

Prayers and sacrifices were common elements in first-century journeys—ways to cope with the dangers of travel. The average traveler promised their gods offerings and sacrifices in return for safety. Roadside shrines also gave travelers opportunities to pray to the local gods for protection. Similarly, the second missionary journey began with a blessing in the church in Antioch. A day's walk with Paul, Silas, and Timothy would surely include prayer along the way.[4] Travelers also paid attention to dreams and omens for guidance and warnings of danger. The Holy Spirit's intervention and Paul's vision in Acts 16:6–10 would not have seemed out of place.

As a day on the road came to an end, travelers would start looking for lodging. Public inns usually had a tavern and three or four shared bedrooms, and they often rented out slaves as prostitutes. Inns were not highly regarded. Complaints describe lice and fleas, the danger of fire, and unscrupulous innkeepers who overcharged and even robbed their guests. Travelers might instead ask for accommodation in a private home.[5] Whenever possible, people preferred to stay with friends or family. On the second missionary journey, Paul often stayed with the Christian community: Lydia in Philippi, Jason in Thessalonica, and Priscilla and Aquila in Corinth.[6]

As they journeyed across Asia Minor and around the Aegean Sea, Paul and his companions were just one more band of travelers, facing the same hardships as everyone else. They would have been surrounded with the life of the Empire, even if Acts doesn't tell us much about their days on the road.

JOSEPH R. DODSON

ACTS 16:6–40

WHO'S CALLING?

CURIOSITY, SUSPENSE, & SURPRISE IN ACTS 16

The deadline had arrived. I paced my office praying for a sign. If I stepped out to relocate my family to Scotland, would the Lord provide? Although I had once been certain he had called me to make the move, the lack of financial support caused significant doubt.

I grew up in a Christian tradition that discouraged asking God for signs. Such a request was considered, at best, a demonstration of distrust and, at worst, a violation of the "Don't test the Lord your God" command. But desperate times called for drastic measures—even if they came from other denominations. So, against my upbringing, I did it. I asked God for a sign.

I can't remember how long it was after my petition that I heard a knock on the door. I figured it was one of the many transients who called on our church's food pantry. When I opened the door, I could tell from the looks of him I had guessed correctly. I was ready to get rid of the guy so I could get back to discerning the Lord's will for my life. I didn't even give him a chance to speak. I just waved him inside and led him to the bags of rice and cans of beans.

After I loaded him up with nonperishables, he spoke up to thank me. When I heard his accent, my jaw dropped. Although I had served countless transients, I had never heard one of them sound like this. Wide-eyed, I blurted: "Where are you from?" As if he got that a lot, he smiled a toothy grin and boasted with a thick brogue: "I moved here from Scotland."

A CURIOUS VISION

While I cannot say whether this man was my sign from the Lord, it reminds me of when, to direct Paul's steps, God sent the apostle a sign—a vision of a man from Macedonia. In Acts 16, as Paul sets his course during the second missionary journey, the Lord keeps turning him back. The Spirit prevents him from going to the province of Asia and then does not allow him to enter Bithynia, either. But then one night in Troas, Paul has a dream.

> *During the night Paul had a vision of a [certain] man of Macedonia standing and begging him, "Come over to Macedonia and help us." After Paul had seen the vision, we got ready at once to leave for Macedonia, concluding that God had called us to preach the gospel to them.* (Acts 16:9–10 NIV) [1]

Curiosity always gets the best of me when I read this account. Who was this Macedonian man? Why didn't Luke tell us? Did he not know? Did he not care? Or was the man's identity an inside joke between Luke and his audience?

It has been suggested that, for the original audience, Paul's vision would have conjured up the image of the most notorious Macedonian, Alexander the Great.[2] Like Paul, Alexander had a guiding vision[3] and dared to cross ethnic lines in an attempt to unite the world by a common culture.[4] It also has been proposed that the man in Paul's vision was Luke himself—the writer making a cameo appearance (in the style of Alfred Hitchcock, perhaps, or Stan Lee).

Moving beyond these conjectures, I've since learned that literary critics look for the use of rhetorical tools such as curiosity, suspense, and surprise as universal techniques in narratives.[5] The more I dive into that research, the more I suspect that Luke was employing these timeless tools of storytelling. That is to say, it is possible that Luke's lack of detail regarding the man in Paul's vision is meant partly to pique our curiosity.

A STRING OF SURPRISES

According to scholars, authors often use "strategic obscuring" to raise questions in the minds of their audience.[6] Once evoked, "curiosity ... lingers and pulls our mind backward while we go forward"; it then creates suspense that "arises whenever we look ahead to a resolution."[7]

As readers go forward in Acts 16, they are placed on tenterhooks waiting to see if the identity of the man will be disclosed once Paul arrives in Macedonia. Further, perhaps the audience's suspense gives way to surprise—since, when Paul first arrives in Philippi, he meets not a man of Macedonia but a woman of Thyatira!

Luke may be using the rhetorical tools of curiosity, suspense, and surprise to underline a common theme in his works: the importance of women in the kingdom of God.[8] Lydia becomes pivotal to Paul's mission, serving as his patroness and provider as he founds the Philippian church.[9] What's more, perhaps Luke intends to continue building suspense and causing surprise with Paul's next encounter—which, again, is not with a man, but with a demon-possessed girl.

If so, Luke eventually gives the audience the resolution they've been seeking: Toward the end of Paul's time in Philippi, he finally shares the gospel with a man in Macedonia. Yet Luke seems to have another surprise in hand. Paul encounters this man not down by the river with the Godfearers, but in jail surrounded by criminals.

Having told of Paul's flogging and imprisonment for exorcising the girl's demon, Luke applies more layers of curiosity, suspense, and surprise as he describes the outcome. In the face of severe injustice and abuse, the apostles astonishingly

PAUL'S VISION

"The Vision of the Macedonian," fresco at the basilica of Saint Paul Outside the Walls in Rome

respond by singing praises to the Lord. Immediately comes another surprise: an earthquake rocks the place and sets the captives free. Next, suspense intensifies as the jailer reaches for his sword to commit suicide. But Paul interrupts the attempt with an amazing revelation: none of the prisoners had run away! Surprisingly, the jailer and his whole household get baptized. The joy of the event is punctuated by a spontaneous celebration meal—in the middle of the night!

A SIGN FROM GOD?

In comparison with Acts 16, I cannot say for sure that my Scottish visitor was a sign. However, I can testify from experience that—as seen in Acts—God faithfully guides his followers' steps, provides for their needs, and surprises them with marvelous encounters.

For instance, two weeks after that knock on the door, the Lord brought another stranger into my life who, out of the blue, wrote a check to cover my entire tuition—for three years no less.

Soli deo gloria!

TIMOTHY GOMBIS

ACTS 16:11–40

DEFAMED & VINDICATED IN A ROMAN COLONY

Paul and Silas arrived in Philippi after traveling from Troas through Samothrace and Neapolis. Located on the northern shore of the Aegean Sea, Philippi was founded by Alexander the Great's father, Philip, in the fourth century BC, and several centuries later the Roman emperor Octavian settled army veterans there (during the first century BC).

Luke emphasizes the Roman character of Philippi by mentioning that it was a Roman colony and then noting (three times) that the events at Philippi unfolded among people who were Romans. This detail provides significant interpretive context for two of the events that occur.

As he did in other places, Paul began his gospel ministry at Philippi among Jews. On the Sabbath, he and Silas went to a spot along the river where they expected to find a "place of prayer"—likely a reference to a synagogue. He encountered some women who had gathered there and found a welcome hearing for the gospel, especially in the case of one woman, Lydia. She was a Godfearer, which means she was a gentile who sympathized with the Jewish faith and worshiped the God of Israel. The church in Philippi originated by meeting in her house.

TYRIAN PURPLE

A predatory sea snail was commonly used to create this costly purple dye. Lydia, who hosted Paul and the believers at Philippi, is described as "a merchant dealing in purple cloth" (Acts 16:14).

> BY REVEALING THE MISSIONARIES' INTENTIONS, THE SLAVE GIRL WAS RUINING THEIR OPPORTUNITY TO PREACH THE GOSPEL.

DEFAMED AS CRIMINALS

Trouble erupts when Paul and Silas encounter a slave girl who was possessed by a spirit of divination and who was making money for her owners by predicting the future. She followed the missionaries around, proclaiming that "these men are servants of the Most High God, who are telling you the way to be saved" (Acts 16:17).[1] In trying to understand the reason behind Paul's response to the girl, interpreters may be tempted to find some fault with what she was saying—as though Paul grew annoyed because she was deceiving the public. But this is not the case.

The generic term "Most High God" was known to cultures in the ancient world as the god who stands over and rules the pantheon of deities. It was a term used to speak either of the chief deity or the god of a certain nation. In such contexts, a nation would claim this title for its own god as the one who not only ruled over that nation but reigned supreme over the deities of all nations. The Old Testament sometimes speaks in this way about the God of Israel. For instance, the Israelites confessed that Yahweh alone was "the Most High over all the earth; you are exalted far above all gods" (Psalm 97:9).

The slave girl, therefore, was reliably representing the truth of Paul and Silas' mission. Why, then, does Luke state that Paul "became so annoyed" that he commanded the spirit to leave her (Acts 16:18)? Given Luke's emphasis on the Roman context, it is likely that Roman values associated with its honor/shame culture are in play.

One of the virtues of honor was decorum, which in Roman public life was manifested by the way a person carried himself, including his posture, speech, and ability to respond well to a polite greeting or even an insult. A virtuous person—one who had decorum—was regarded as having divine favor, and Paul and Silas were trying to conduct themselves well in order to gain a hearing for the gospel. If another person revealed your intentions before you could build credibility and reveal them on your own terms, you would lose face and be regarded as dishonorable. So by revealing the missionaries' intentions, the slave girl was shaming them and ruining their opportunity to preach the gospel. In order to preserve their credibility, Paul cast out the spirit from the girl.

This, of course, enraged the girl's owners, who were upset over their economic loss. After they accused the missionaries of unlawful conduct, the city magistrates had Paul and Silas beaten and thrown into prison. This would have sent the whole city the message that these foreigners were behaving criminally.

VINDICATED AS CITIZENS

That night an earthquake shook loose the prisoners' bonds and opened the doors to the jail. Thinking that everyone had gone free, the jailer—who was responsible for containing the prisoners—was about to kill himself out of shame. Paul, however, notified him that all the prisoners were still in the jail, so there was no need for him to die. This led to the jailer confessing Christ and gathering his household into the movement of those who were following Jesus.

What happened next calls for explanation. The next day, the city magistrates told the jailer to release the prisoners, and the jailer passed this information to Paul and

PAUL IN CHAINS

Accused of unlawful conduct, Paul and Silas were thrown in jail at Philippi.

Silas, thinking that they would be happy to depart in peace. But Paul refused to go quietly. He demanded that the city magistrates come and escort them out publicly. He noted that he and Silas were Roman citizens, which made it an imperial offense for them to be so badly treated.

This might be taken as an indication that Paul was insisting on his rights, protesting the suffering he endured for his loyalty to Jesus. But this view creates some tension with Paul's willingness elsewhere to suffer for the cause of Christ, and even to invite others to endure suffering.[2] Here in Acts 16, Paul once again is operating out of concern for the gospel rather than personal vindication.

The missionaries' public beating associated the gospel of Christ with criminal activity, and Paul was eager to set the record straight. He did not care that he had to suffer for being a Christian minister. His concern was to vindicate the gospel, and he used his Roman citizenship to do so. He was not insisting on his own rights. In fact, elsewhere Paul reveals his regular ministry strategy as refusing to assert the rights he knows are his by virtue of being an apostle.[3] As servants of Jesus Christ, Paul and Silas had not behaved badly, and the public act of the magistrates escorting them from jail would have protected the remaining Christians from any suspicion.

Throughout the narrative, the Roman context of the events in Philippi help to make sense of what Luke records. What happens in this episode is indicative of a pattern seen elsewhere in Acts: the apostles are regarded as upsetting the Roman social order and behaving unlawfully, but when they are examined, they are vindicated as behaving righteously.

CARYN A. REEDER

ACTS 17:1–15

TURNING THE WORLD UPSIDE DOWN

In Philippi, Paul and Silas are accused of disturbing the city. These charges result in a night in prison before they leave for Thessalonica. Paul spent the next three Sabbaths in the local synagogue in Thessalonica, explaining and teaching from Scripture that the Messiah had to suffer, die, and be raised from the dead, and proclaiming that Jesus is this Messiah. According to Acts 17:4, Paul persuaded some Jews, many Greeks who worshiped God, and women who were leaders in the community. But even three carefully argued sermons could not convince everyone. Some of the Thessalonians accuse Paul and Silas not of disturbing the city alone, but of upsetting the whole world.

FOR PAUL TO NAME JESUS AS KING WAS TO DEFY THE EMPEROR.

OPPOSITION TO THE GOSPEL

Some of the unpersuaded Jews are described as jealous. This might mean they were envious of Paul's influence, but the same description is used for the zeal that led Paul to persecute the church.[1] The unpersuaded Jews in Thessalonica may have been zealous against what they saw as heresy in Paul's message. Whatever their motivation, the unpersuaded Jews gathered "wicked men" from the marketplace to disrupt the city. When they could not find Paul, the mob dragged Jason (Paul's host) and other believers before the local authorities.

In Acts 17:6, the mob identifies Paul and Silas as people who were upsetting the whole world. The Greek verb for "upsetting" also can be translated as "rebelling" or "revolting," and "the whole world" was a common way of describing the Roman Empire. The mob, in other words, was accusing Paul and Silas of instigating a revolt against the Empire, as the additional claims in Acts 17:7 make clear: by announcing Jesus as king, Paul and Silas were acting against the decrees of Caesar.

The charges at Thessalonica intensified the accusations brought by the owners of the slave girl in Philippi. They had claimed Paul and Silas were troublemakers—Jews who proclaimed customs unlawful for Romans (Acts 16:19–21). The Philippian authorities had Paul and Silas stripped, beaten, and imprisoned overnight. In Thessalonica, the authorities were concerned enough to make Jason and the other believers pay bail as a guarantee of good behavior before releasing them.

In contrast to these events in Philippi and Thessalonica, a tribunal in Corinth refused to take up charges brought against Paul, saying it was a Jewish matter of no concern to Romans (Acts 18:12–13). This response may seem natural to readers familiar with the "separation of church and state," and we might wonder how the charges in Philippi and Thessalonica succeeded. But the reason the accusers in Corinth were not successful has to do with their framing of the case, not with the government's disinterest in religious matters. If they had focused on Paul's challenge to Roman law, the accusation might have stood.

THE THREAT OF THE GOSPEL

Across the Empire, worship, prayer, and sacrifice were part of daily life. Families made regular offerings of incense and food to household gods. Temples were not just places of worship; they also served as public meeting rooms, banks, and storehouses for official documents. Images of the gods decorated streets, markets, and bathhouses.

Religion also was integral to the Roman Empire as a political entity. The Senate met in temples, opening their gatherings with sacrifices and auspices (interpreting natural signs to determine the gods' will). Military action began and ended with prayer and sacrifice, and the legions carried images of their gods into battle on their standards. The emperor was the pontifex maximus—the primary priest of Rome. He also was considered to be divine, and living and dead emperors were worshiped across the Empire. In Paul's day, the imperial cult unified the provinces around the emperor as god, priest, and father of his people.

The integration of religious belief and practice into all aspects of life, including politics, helps explain the accusations brought against the believers in Acts. The Romans valued tradition. Disasters from fire to famine to war were often blamed on the neglect of the gods, and the restoration of worship was associated with victory and peace. Christianity disrupted traditional religion. For the Romans, Christians were a dangerous threat to local and imperial prosperity. Their refusal to worship the gods—including the emperor—was treason.[2]

Therefore, whatever their motivation, the mob in Thessalonica was not entirely wrong to use the language of political rebellion in their accusations. For Paul to name Jesus as king was to defy the emperor. Of course, to be Messiah was not quite

ROMAN EMPEROR

The emperor was the pontifex maximus—the primary priest of Rome. He also was considered to be divine, and living and dead emperors were worshiped across the Empire.

Marble bust of Tiberius, emperor of Rome from AD 14 to 37

the same as being emperor, and Jesus' kingdom was not precisely a political threat to Rome. However, Jesus' kingdom was theologically opposed to imperial values. If Paul's message took hold, it would replace the emperor—the god, father, and priest of his people—with Jesus; imperial decrees with the gospel; power and status with mutual servanthood; and imperial violence with self-sacrifice.[3]

THE ADVANCE OF THE GOSPEL

The accusations against Paul, Silas, and the other believers in Thessalonica make sense in the context of the Roman Empire. At the same time, it is actually the accusers who upset civic order by recruiting a mob and invading Jason's house.[4] In contrast, Jason and the other believers obeyed the authorities, and Paul walked away from his accusers rather than fighting back. Paul, Jason, and the others followed the example of Jesus, proving their innocence against their accusers.[5]

Just as Jesus' accusers failed to end his story, the mob in Thessalonica failed to silence the gospel. Ironically, they prompted its spread by forcing Paul and Silas to move on to Berea—where their message was eagerly received—and then to Athens. Despite the mob's opposition, the church in Thessalonica grew. Later, in his letter to the believers there, Paul praised them as an example to others for enduring persecution with faith and joy.[6]

The revolutionary message of the gospel could not be stopped.

DAMASCUS
ANTIOCH
CYPRUS
PAPHOS
PISIDIAN ANTIOCH
LYSTRA
TROAS
PHILIPPI
THESSALONICA
ATHENS

ANDREW SUTHERLAND

ACTS 17:16–34

PREACHING CHRIST IN A PLACE WITH MANY GODS

When Paul went to Athens, he might as well have stepped into a time machine and taken a trans-Atlantic flight. There, in the intellectual heart of ancient Greece, Paul found himself in a culture uncannily similar to that of our own 21st-century United States.

Images of innumerable gods surrounded him. People of different faiths, from Jewish to pagan, inhabited the city. These religious differences were tolerated in Athens—which, after all, was regarded as the cultural and intellectual apex of the first-century world (much like New York City today). With their refined worldview, the Athenians happily tolerated diversity in religious faith. In fact, they

PAUL'S MESSAGE WAS MORE THAN JUST ANOTHER INTERESTING IDEA; IT REQUIRED A CHANGE OF DIRECTION.

made it a source of entertainment, priding themselves on mastering the latest and most exotic ways of thinking.[1] The people of Athens would spend all day doing so (see Acts 17:21).

In this pluralistic society, many different faiths abounded, but no faith held the center. The focus and guide of daily life was human achievement—namely, the

THE ACROPOLIS AT ATHENS

The focus and guide of daily life was human achievement—namely, the Athenians' democracy, culture, and intellectual advancement.

Leo von Klenze, "The Acropolis at Athens" (1846)

Athenians' democracy, culture, and intellectual advancement. Religion was at best a secondary consideration, something that fit into the reigning way of life rather than establishing it.

The challenge Paul faced as a missionary in Athens parallels one that faces American Christians today: preaching the gospel in a place where all religions are treated as equals. And though the Athenians who heard Paul did not exactly line up to be baptized, his approach provides a helpful model of what to do and what to expect in our own efforts to share the gospel.

BUILDING A BRIDGE

Paul addresses the Athenians at the Areopagus, a hill of bare rock used for centuries as a meeting place for councils and courts. (The Greek name means

"Ares Hill," rendered in Latin as "Mars Hill.") He begins by finding the best in his audience. This could not have been easy; the city's many idols "greatly distressed" him (Acts 17:16). Nonetheless, Paul opens his speech by complementing the Athenians for being "extremely religious"—and this was not mere flattery (Acts 17:22–23). As theologian Will Willimon writes, the altar to the unknown God shows that the Athenians yearned for the God whom only the Scriptures could disclose.[2]

Paul sees this yearning, and he uses it to create a bridge between his audience and the gospel: what the Athenians seek but cannot name is the one true God. This God made the world, needs nothing from humans, and gave life to all humankind. Certain strands of Greek philosophy already contained similar ideas of a creator god and taught that the gods had no needs. So by starting with commonalities, Paul eases his audience into his message.

Throughout the speech, Paul works to maintain this bridge. He even cites a Greek poet in support of his claims. And even though Paul's thought is clearly informed by the Old Testament, he does not quote it directly, which could have alienated his non-Jewish audience. He simply alludes to parts of Scripture, such as the story of Adam.

ANNOUNCING THE TRUTH

For all his interest in finding common ground, Paul does not contort his message to fit into the culture of Athens. He ultimately preaches that God calls people everywhere to repent, that Jesus will righteously judge the world, and that Jesus has been raised from the dead.

Because of his message, some of Paul's listeners scoff—particularly at his claim about the resurrection. Indeed, the idea of resurrection was as utterly contrary to first-century Greek philosophy as it is to 21st-century science. But resurrection was probably just the final straw. Worshiping only one God also would have been foreign to Greek thought, and the claim that God calls all people to repent made Paul's message more than just another interesting idea to contemplate; it required a change of direction.

Many of the Athenians shut Paul out—a response we ought to expect. In a world where religions are treated as nothing more than sets of ideas and preferences, claims that there is one true God and that Jesus will judge the whole world will seldom be received well.

But the rejection is not total. Though some Athenians scoff, others take a middle ground, promising to hear Paul again. And a few even become believers.

Paul's words to the Athenians give us wise insights for sharing the message of Christ in our own context: there is value in finding the best in our skeptical audience, building a bridge to the gospel using human yearning and shared beliefs, and ultimately preaching the heart of the gospel boldly. And the Areopagus speech is not the only model Scripture provides us. Earlier in Acts, for instance, we see a completely different approach in Stephen's speech to non-Christian Jews (Acts 7:2–53). Taken together, both episodes advise us to understand our audience and choose our approach strategically.

The Athenians' reactions to Paul show that when God's word is proclaimed, some will believe and some will mock. That is just the nature of things in a pluralistic society. But regardless of the success rate and whatever our context, we must preach.

DAVID B. SCHREINER

ACTS 18:1–17

PAUL'S BOOMTOWN

The city of Corinth was one of the great urban centers of antiquity, with a history reaching back to the Neolithic period. Strabo, a Greek historian and geographer who lived in the first centuries BC and AD, described Corinth as "always great and wealthy."[1]

The Corinth of Strabo's day—and Paul's—was a Roman creation. Sacked by Rome in 146 BC, the city lay vacant for a century until Julius Caesar rebuilt it into a Roman colony (44 BC). Once the infrastructure was in place, diverse peoples rapidly populated the city. New Testament scholar Scott J. Hafemann describes first-century Corinth as a "boomtown," and it eventually became one of the most influential cities in the Roman Empire.[2]

A key aspect of Corinth's influence was its incredibly strategic location on a narrow isthmus linking the Greek mainland with the Peloponnesian peninsula. From this position, the city controlled two harbors connected by a paved road, across which cargo and boats could be transported from one harbor to the other. Corinth had a bustling city center with markets, administrative centers, and

JUDGING FROM PAUL'S LETTERS, CORINTH WAS PERHAPS HIS MOST CHALLENGING MINISTRY.

leisure spots, making it a major stop on the Roman roadway system. The city even hosted the Isthmian Games every two years.

For all of these reasons, Corinth became a melting pot of ideas, cultures, and resources. This cosmopolitan environment, with a diverse and transient population, was ideal for spreading new teachings and customs. The city's religious life was eclectically pagan. Excavations have revealed prominent worship centers

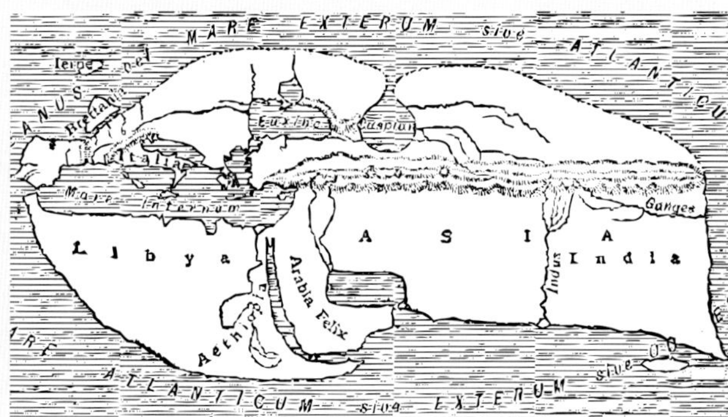

STRABO

Strabo was a Greek geographer and historian who lived during Paul's time. He described the city of Corinth as "always great and wealthy."

Strabo in a 16th-century engraving and his map of the world as published in Encyclopaedia Biblica *(1903)*

devoted to the imperial cult, Athena, Aphrodite, and more. There also was a notable Jewish population at Corinth, evidenced by an inscription designating the city's synagogue.

Corinth's tightly packed religious scene sheds light on one of the more curious episodes of Paul's ministry in the city. He regularly argued in the synagogue, but eventually he was compelled to "shake off the dust" and shift his focus away from the Jews (Acts 18:4–6). But instead of going across town, Paul merely went next door, to the home of Titius Justus. Why next door? It's not clear. Suggestions range from happenstance to indirect persuasion and competition. What's clear is that Paul's missional shift did not amount to a clean break from ministry among the Jews. Acts 18:8 recounts how the leader of the synagogue, Crispus, and his entire household, soon came down the street to worship with the Christians. Thus, while Paul's focus may have shifted at times based on the Jewish reception, Paul never forgot about his kinsmen.

In Paul's day, Corinth's Hellenistic (Greek) heritage influenced daily life much more than Roman customs. Hafemann suggests that Hellenistic ideals led to competition and factions within the young congregation, producing the conflicts Paul addresses in 1 and 2 Corinthians.[3] Intra-church strife allowed Paul's opponents to sway the congregation and challenge his authority and teaching, reflecting a major concern of 2 Corinthians.

Judging from Paul's letters, Corinth was perhaps his most challenging ministry. The booming city's diversity led to tension and division in the church—making Paul's teachings on unity and love all the more significant.[4] The church in first-century Corinth may be a helpful model for our own churches today, as we strive to bridge our differences and bear witness to the gospel as one body of Christ.

ARCHAEOLOGICAL CONNECTIONS TO CORINTH

CORINTH'S BEMA SEAT

Corinth's bema *seat, or public adjudication site, has been excavated. This was where Paul stood trial in front of Gallio (Acts 18:12–17). According to an inscription from Delphi, Gallio served as proconsul during* AD *51–52. This detail that has allowed scholars to date Paul's ministry in Corinth with relative certainty.*

CORINTH INSCRIPTION

An inscription found at Corinth bears the name of Erastus, a city administrator who may have been an associate of Paul (Acts 19:22; 2 Timothy 4:20; Romans 16:23).

Sources: "Gallio (Person)," Anchor Bible Dictionary, *ed. David Noel Freedman (New York: Doubleday, 1992), 2:902; "Erastus (Person),"* Anchor Bible Dictionary, *2:571*

CULTIVATING FAITH, NURTURING THE CHURCH

JAMES W. THOMPSON

From the time Paul reaches center stage in Acts until the end of the book, he is a traveler. In his three missionary journeys and final trip to Jerusalem, he travels to fulfill his mission of preaching Jesus Christ; later he travels to Rome as a prisoner. In Luke's portrayal of the missionary journeys, Paul's preaching consistently calls for a decision, and he leaves each city with some converts and considerable opposition. Under these conditions, the converts are left in a precarious position.

Since the focus of Acts is on the travel and missionary preaching of Paul, it provides little information about the future of the churches that Paul left behind or about his pastoral activities with new believers. Luke does not mention that Paul wrote letters to the churches, and he provides only rare glimpses of the task of nurturing churches. During the first missionary journey, Paul and his team retraced their route and returned to the churches they had established in Lystra, Iconium, and Pisidian Antioch, where they "strengthened the souls of the disciples and encouraged them to remain in the faith," reminding them that "it is through many persecutions that we must enter the kingdom of God" (Acts 14:22).[1]

At the beginning of the second missionary journey, Paul and Silas went through Syria and Cilicia, "strengthening the churches" (Acts 15:41). While Luke makes passing mention of the encouragement of new disciples, he gives no indication of how Paul instructed believers after they were baptized. He notes that Paul stayed for extended periods in Corinth (18 months) and Ephesus (two years), but he says little about the formation of the churches. To better understand Paul's nurturing activity, we must turn to the letters he wrote to his fledging congregations.

RELYING ON A TEAM

While Paul was in Corinth, he was rejoined by Silas and Timothy, whom he had left behind in Macedonia to minister to the churches there. Because Paul had left the Thessalonian converts prematurely—and in a precarious situation—he had sent Timothy to "strengthen and encourage [them], so that no one would be shaken by the persecutions" (1 Thessalonians 3:2–3). Later, Timothy arrived in Corinth with a positive report, prompting Paul to write the letter known as 1 Thessalonians. This sequence of events illustrates the means of Paul's pastoral work among his churches. He did not abandon the churches that he had established, but sent coworkers to continue discipling the believers.[2]

Paul also extended his pastoral work by dispatching couriers with letters he wrote for the purpose of comforting, confirming, and encouraging new converts. His letters are substitutes for his own presence—continuations of the pastoral care that he began when he was with the believers. He writes to reinforce what they already know, to correct misunderstandings, to answer questions from his churches, and to correct false teaching.

BUILDING A FAMILY

First Thessalonians offers a significant window into Paul's ministry of forming and nurturing his churches. In this letter, Paul recalls his activities with the believers in the first days after their conversion. Before he was forced to leave Thessalonica, he was deeply involved in the formation of a lasting community. For those whose conversion alienated them from family and other associations, Paul provided a new family—the church.

He describes himself in familial terms, first as a "nurse taking care of her own children" (1 Thessalonians 2:7), then as a father with his children, "encouraging ... urging ... and pleading" for them to walk worthily of their calling (2:12). When he departed from believers, he was "orphaned" and hoped to return to them (2:17). Paul's frequent address to the community as "brothers and sisters" in 1 Thessalonians—as in all of his letters—further indicates the formation of a new family.

Paul called on the new converts to nurture each other, taking the place of the families that had abandoned them because of their faith. His frequent references to "one another" indicate that the care they give each other is an alternative to the care given by their blood relatives. Indeed, to "love one another" is not only to express kind emotions toward others, but to become the social safety net that is normally provided by families.

FOR THOSE WHOSE CONVERSION ALIENATED THEM FROM FAMILY AND OTHER ASSOCIATIONS, PAUL PROVIDED A NEW FAMILY—**THE CHURCH.**

TEACHING THE GOSPEL

The task of community formation went beyond strengthening social bonds and involved instructing the believers about the gospel. Paul's efforts to provide sound teaching are evident in 1 Thessalonians, where he frequently refers to what his converts already knew:

- "You yourselves know that we were destined for [persecutions]" (3:3).
- "We told you beforehand that we will suffer persecutions" (3:4).
- "For you know what instructions we gave you" (4:2).
- "God is an avenger as we told you beforehand" (4:5).
- "You have been taught by God to love one another" (4:9).
- "You yourselves know that the day of the Lord will come as a thief" (5:2).

Similarly, during Paul's stay in Corinth, he engaged in extensive instruction for new converts about the conduct of public worship and about the fundamentals of the faith.[3] His frequent questions starting with "Do you not know?" indicate that he instructed the community on moral expectations for believers.

MAKING DISCIPLES

Paul continued his pastoral care in his own return visits to his churches.[4] His ultimate goal was not just to make converts, but to initiate a process of Christian formation among his churches that would continue until Christ returned. Paul portrays himself both as the father of the bride, with the aim of presenting the church as a pure virgin to Christ (2 Corinthians 11:2), and as the expectant mother who is in birth pangs "until Christ is formed among [his churches]" (Galatians 4:19).

Only if Paul's churches are "blameless" at the day of Christ will he know that he did not "labor in vain."[5] His visits and letters are intended to ensure that his churches will be transformed into the image of Christ.

Portrait of Paul (17th century; artist unknown) in the Convento de San Esteban in Salamanca, Spain

PAUL'S THIRD MISSIONARY JOURNEY

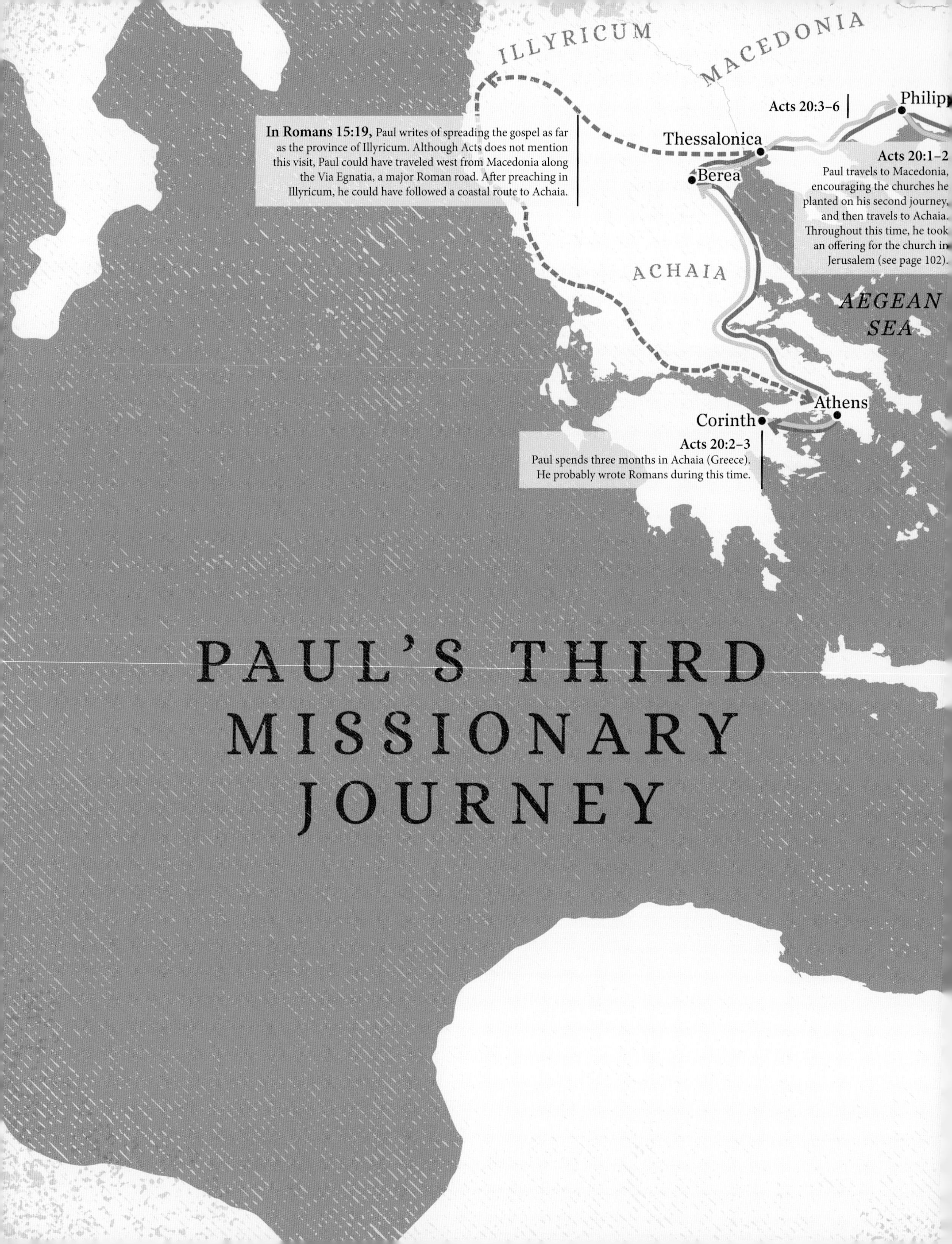

ILLYRICUM

MACEDONIA

ACHAIA

AEGEAN SEA

Philipp

Thessalonica

Berea

Athens

Corinth

Acts 20:3–6

In Romans 15:19, Paul writes of spreading the gospel as far as the province of Illyricum. Although Acts does not mention this visit, Paul could have traveled west from Macedonia along the Via Egnatia, a major Roman road. After preaching in Illyricum, he could have followed a coastal route to Achaia.

Acts 20:1–2
Paul travels to Macedonia, encouraging the churches he planted on his second journey, and then travels to Achaia. Throughout this time, he took an offering for the church in Jerusalem (see page 102).

Acts 20:2–3
Paul spends three months in Achaia (Greece). He probably wrote Romans during this time.

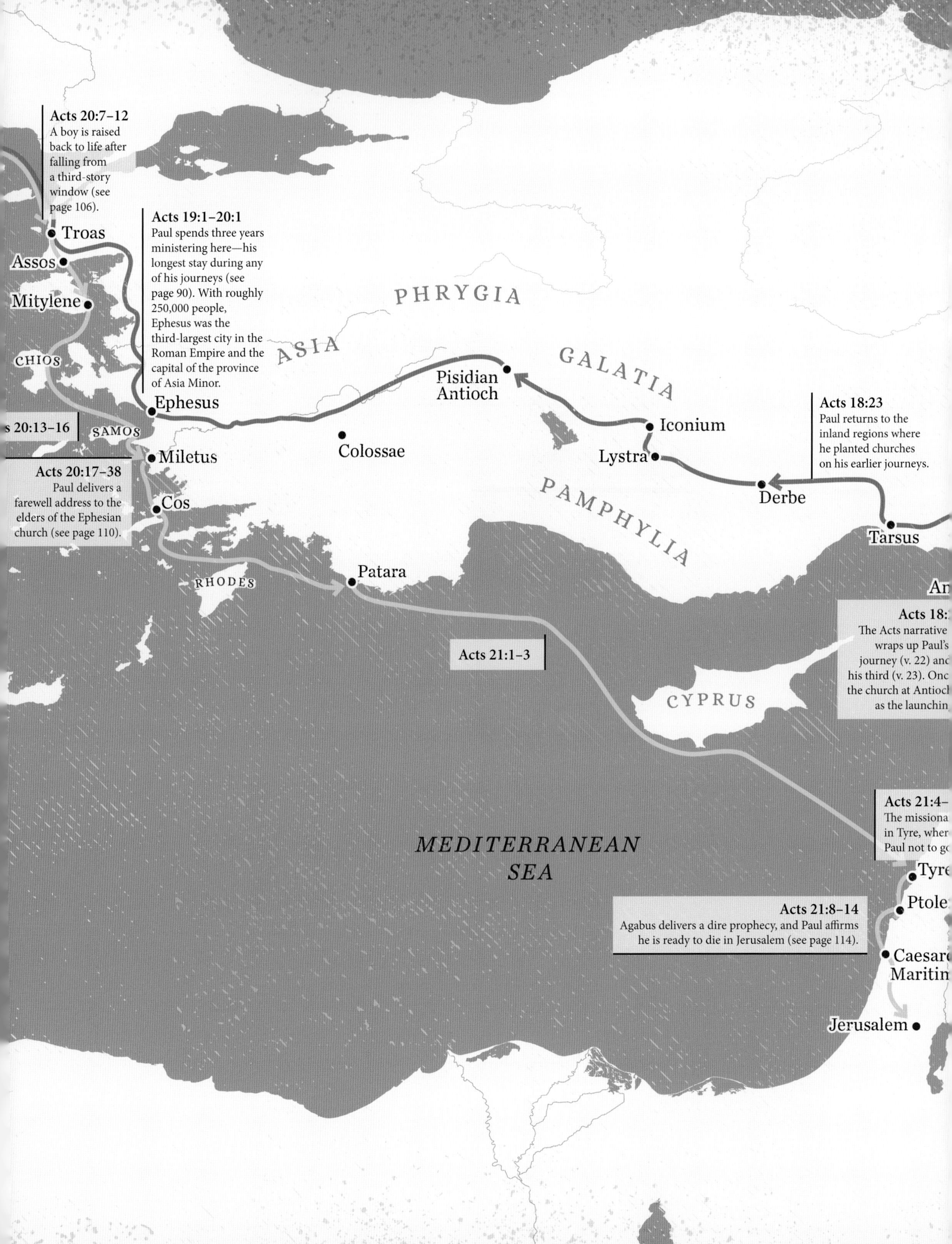

Acts 20:7–12
A boy is raised back to life after falling from a third-story window (see page 106).
Acts 19:1–20:1
Paul spends three years ministering here—his longest stay during any of his journeys (see page 90). With roughly 250,000 people, Ephesus was the third-largest city in the Roman Empire and the capital of the province of Asia Minor.
Troas
Assos
Mitylene
CHIOS
PHRYGIA
ASIA
GALATIA
Pisidian Antioch
Ephesus
s 20:13–16
SAMOS
Miletus
Colossae
Iconium
Lystra
Acts 18:23
Paul returns to the inland regions where he planted churches on his earlier journeys.
Acts 20:17–38
Paul delivers a farewell address to the elders of the Ephesian church (see page 110).
Cos
PAMPHYLIA
Derbe
Tarsus
RHODES
Patara
Acts 21:1–3
CYPRUS
MEDITERRANEAN SEA
Tyre
Acts 21:8–14
Agabus delivers a dire prophecy, and Paul affirms he is ready to die in Jerusalem (see page 114).
Jerusalem

Paul's Travel Companions on the Third Missionary Journey

Acts reports a number of believers joining Paul's third missionary journey. Several might have been appointed by their churches to assist with the collection for the Jerusalem Christians.[1]

Timothy first joined the missionaries when they visited his hometown of Lystra (in Galatia) during the second journey (Acts 16:1–3). He eventually became Paul's right-hand man, often traveling ahead of Paul or representing him to the churches.[2] He is named as co-author on seven of Paul's letters.

Erastus was with Paul in Ephesus. Shortly before the riot there, Paul sent Erastus and Timothy ahead to Macedonia (Acts 19:22).

Aristarchus, from Thessalonica, was caught up in the riot in Ephesus but continued to travel with Paul (Acts 19:29; 20:4). It seems he made the journey to Jerusalem, as he later sailed with Paul to Rome (27:2). At some point, he was imprisoned with Paul (Colossians 4:10).

Gaius was seized by the mob in Ephesus (Acts 19:29). It's not clear whether this was the same Gaius who sailed to Troas (20:4). The first man is described as a Macedonian, while the second is said to be from the city of Derbe in Galatia.

Tychicus and **Trophimus**, from Asia Minor, are named among those who sailed to Troas—likely traveling ahead of the main group to make preparations (Acts 20:4–5). Tychicus was the courier who delivered Paul's letters to the Ephesians and Colossians (Ephesians 6:21–22; Colossians 4:7–8). He was enough of a leader in the church to represent Paul's ministry (Titus 3:12; 2 Timothy 4:12).

Luke—traditionally accepted as the author of Acts—apparently traveled with Paul from Philippi to Jerusalem and later to Rome (see page 56).

Other companions include **Sopater**, from Berea, and **Secundus**, from Thessalonica (Acts 20:4).

Compiled from Lexham Bible Dictionary

THE THIRD MISSIONARY JOURNEY

ACTS 18:23–21:14

PRESSING ON WITH THE MISSION

Much of Paul's third westward journey remains unknown to us. His ministry to the churches in Galatia and Macedonia fly by in a single verse for each region (Acts 18:23; 20:2), and his three-month stay in Achaia (Greece) is mentioned only in passing, as the turnaround point of the journey. It seems that Luke, the presumed author of Acts, wasn't interested in these stages of Paul's mission—perhaps because he was retracing his route from the second journey.

Instead, Luke focuses the third journey's narrative on a place Paul had not yet visited—Ephesus, a cosmopolitan port city perched on the western edge of the province of Asia (modern-day Turkey). Paul spent three years in Ephesus, making this the longest stay of his missionary career. His ministry was effective enough to spark a large riot among the city's silversmiths, who earned a living off pagan idolatry.

Despite the gaps in Luke's account, we get a fuller picture of the third journey from details in Paul's letters:

Paul might have taken a longer route. In Romans 15:19, Paul claims to have spread the gospel as far as Illyricum, northwest of Macedonia. Many scholars think Paul made this trip on his way to Achaia (during the long journey covered in 20:2).

Paul was busy writing. Clues within several of Paul's letters suggest they were written during the third journey.[1] Scholars generally agree that Paul penned 1 Corinthians during his time in Ephesus and 2 Corinthians sometime after reaching Macedonia. Once he arrived in Achaia (Corinth), he almost certainly used this three-month stay during the winter to write his lengthy letter to the Romans.

Paul was taking up a collection. First and Second Corinthians and Romans all refer to an offering Paul was collecting from the churches of Galatia, Macedonia, and Achaia.[2] Many interpreters believe the traveling companions named in Acts 20:4 were representatives chosen by local churches to help Paul deliver their monetary gifts to the impoverished Christians in Jerusalem.

The work of the collection, along with Paul's tearful farewell speech in Miletus, suggest he knew his ministry in this region was drawing to a close. He had succeeded in spreading the gospel to gentiles all around the Aegean shoreline. Now he was ready for the next stage of his mission.

LYNN H. COHICK

ACTS 19

SHAKING THE FOUNDATIONS

PAUL'S MESSAGE BRINGS A SEISMIC CULTURAL SHIFT

The account of Paul's time in Ephesus provides a snapshot of various ministry challenges he faced during his life. The common denominator of these experiences is the revolutionary power of the gospel. The Holy Spirit transformed believers, the power of God worked to heal and to exorcise demons, and the truth of the gospel shook the foundations of a stronghold of paganism.

Paul first visited Ephesus toward the end of his second missionary journey, having sailed across the Aegean Sea from Corinth with his coworkers Priscilla and Aquila. Although Paul did not stay long in Ephesus, he promised the Jews there that he would return and continue the conversation about the Messiah Jesus (Acts 18:19–21). Priscilla and Aquila remained in Ephesus, while Paul continued to Jerusalem and then to Syrian Antioch. Later, on his third journey, Paul passed through southern Asia Minor (modern Turkey) and returned to Ephesus—fulfilling his promise to the Jews. He remained for about three years, the longest period Paul spent in any city around the Aegean.

PAUL'S TEACHINGS ON THE GOSPEL WERE PERSUASIVE, AND GOD'S POWER WAS DEMONSTRATED BY HEALINGS.

A POWERFUL MESSAGE

When Paul returned to Ephesus, he found some "disciples" who knew about the baptism of John, but not about the Holy Spirit. In this, they resemble Apollos, another Jewish-Christian teacher like Paul (see below: "Who Was Apollos?"). However, Apollos did know the story of Jesus (Acts 18:25). This distinction is important, for although Priscilla and Aquila taught Apollos about the Christian faith, they were building on his sound foundation.

The "disciples" at Ephesus could have been followers of John the Baptist—believers who had received a baptism of repentance and awaited the coming Messiah. In Acts 19, Paul announces to these disciples that the Messiah is here—in Jesus. Convinced by Paul's message, they receive the Holy Spirit as they are baptized in Jesus's name.

Three details are worth noting. First, there were 12 men. The number 12 indicates a connection with the tribes of Israel and Jesus' apostles. Second, these

"Epaphroditus, Sosthenes, Apollos, Cephas, and Caesar" (15th century, artist unknown)

WHO WAS APOLLOS?

Acts 18:24–28 introduces a Jewish-Christian teacher named Apollos, who is described as having deep knowledge of the Scriptures (meaning the Old Testament), strong rhetorical skills, and passion for the gospel. Luke identifies Apollos as a native of Alexandria, Egypt, which was a cultural and educational center in the Greco-Roman world. He likely would have been raised in a context of Jewish and Greek scholarship.

Before Paul arrived in Ephesus, Apollos taught in the synagogue there but was not aware of baptism in Christ. Priscilla and Aquila—whom Paul had taught on the second missionary journey—expanded Apollos' understanding of early Christian teaching. With support from the Ephesian church, Apollos went on to teach the believers in Corinth and, according to Luke, was very effective there.

In 1 Corinthians 3, when discussing the problem of factions in the church, Paul refers to Apollos and some believers who apparently aligned with him. To be clear, Paul does not criticize Apollos or imply he was causing division in the church; rather, he argues that Christians should not attach themselves to a particular teacher (which was a common practice among Greek philosophical schools). Another reference to Apollos in Titus 3:13 suggests that he and Paul remained associates for years.

Compiled from Lexham Bible Dictionary

men were Jews living in the diaspora (the Jewish community outside Judea). In Acts, the geographical spread of the gospel is theologically significant. These diaspora Jews, speaking in tongues and prophesying, were part of the gospel's movement from Jerusalem ultimately to Rome (Acts 1:8). Third, Paul lays hands on these disciples, demonstrating his role in manifesting God's power—which becomes evident in other ways as the chapter unfolds.

Paul's powerful teaching persuades some, but after three months in the synagogue, other Jews have had enough, and Paul leaves the synagogue to teach daily in a public venue. The lecture hall of Tyrannus was probably located in the commercial marketplace. This part of Ephesus would have been filled with merchants and orators—everyone who engaged in the life of the busy city—as well as a vast number of visitors to the great temple of Artemis. These people took Paul's gospel message when they returned to their local towns and villages. One example is Epaphras, who returned to his hometown of Colossae (a three-day walk from Ephesus) and founded a church there.

THE GODDESS ARTEMIS

In ancient Greek religion and myth, Artemis (daughter of Zeus and Leto) is the goddess of the hunt, the wilderness, wild animals, the Moon, and chastity. Artemis was the patron and protector of young girls and was believed to bring disease upon women and relieve them of it. Artemis was worshipped as one of the primary goddesses of childbirth and midwifery.

Bust of Artemis, Rome (fourth century BC, artist unknown)

This phase of Paul's ministry lasted about two years—perhaps sponsored by wealthy gentiles interested in the gospel message or even the Asiarchs (Paul's "friends" or patrons who later protect him from the rioting mob). Paul's teachings on the gospel were persuasive, and God's power was demonstrated by healings. The account in Acts 19:11–20 provides evidence that Jesus, and not magic, is the supreme authority over all things in heaven and earth. Luke confirms this in two ways. First, he shows that the power of healing is not generated by Paul himself, for even handkerchiefs taken from Paul (perhaps without his knowledge) convey the healing power about which he preaches. Second, demons who wreak havoc in people's lives confess that they fear Jesus's name, and they know Paul as one who faithfully preaches Jesus.

The Holy Spirit cannot be bought or controlled through incantations, as the sons of Sceva learned to their great harm. Magic was associated with the goddess Artemis in Ephesus; a special incantation engraved in the base of her statue was thought to protect devotees from demons. Believers in Jesus publicly renounced their reliance on such magic, demonstrating the transformational power of the gospel and the expectations of a holy community dedicated to Christ Jesus.

A VIOLENT REACTION

Luke interrupts the story briefly to foreshadow Paul's continuing travels (Acts 19:21–22). In verse 23, he returns to describing the powerful impact of Paul's message, this time stressing the results on the pagan economy. Two important gentile nonbelievers—a silversmith and the city clerk—speak out about the gospel message, and both point to a danger in the current situation. Ironically, it is Paul's enemy, the silversmith Demetrius, who has a better grasp on the perils that Paul's message creates for paganism.

In his speech in verses 25–27, Demetrius makes two claims based on two historical facts. The first claim is economic: he asserts that his trade—crafting silver items (perhaps models of the temple)—will decline if more people reject Artemis and turn to the true God. Economics and religion were intimately related in Ephesus, which profited greatly from tourism, trade, and banking associated with the temple of Artemis. The Artemisium was one of the seven wonders of the ancient world; it was four times larger than the Parthenon in Athens and controlled roughly 77,000 acres of farmland that produced income for the temple.

Demetrius' second claim is theological: Paul is saying that gods made by human hands are not gods at all. This is likely an accurate summary of Paul's monotheistic teachings, shared by all Jews. The problem, as Demetrius sees it, is that Paul is asking gentiles to embrace monotheism through Jesus the Messiah. These gentiles stop celebrating Artemis and buying her silver shrines, thereby dishonoring the goddess and diminishing the silversmiths' profits. Perhaps Demetrius intuited the

THE TEMPLE OF ARTEMIS

This model of the Temple of Artemis, at Miniatürk Park in Istanbul, Turkey, recreates the probable appearance of the temple.

seismic cultural shift brought by Paul's gospel message, which provided healing for many and the gift of the Holy Spirit for everyone—without cost. New communities of equals in Christ would challenge the hierarchical social structure that supported the worship of Artemis.

The other silversmiths and tradesmen share Demetrius' concerns and rally to the goddess, crying, "Great is Artemis of the Ephesians!" Others in the marketplace hear the commotion, and a mob grabs two of Paul's coworkers. The crowd spills into the city's nearby amphitheater, which could hold about 20,000 to 24,000 people on its benches. This was a life-and-death situation for the missionaries, as mob violence and lynchings were a common worry for minorities in Greco-Roman cities.

Although Paul is prepared to address the crowd—probably seeing an amazing opportunity to proclaim the gospel—both the disciples and certain city leaders dissuade him. The Asiarchs (from the Greek words *Asia* and *archōn,* which means "ruler") were probably Paul's patrons. Should he be charged with causing a riot, the damage to his patrons' honor would be severe—even if he were later exonerated. The crowd's hostility might be why some Jews put forward a spokesman, Alexander, to explain that Paul's group was not part of their synagogue. But once the rioters realize Alexander is Jewish, they shout him down and become more agitated. At this point, the only thing saving the missionaries might be the crowd's confusion about the cause of the riot.

Mob action imperiled not only the lives of Paul and his co-workers, but also the political status of the city. Ephesus was the seat of the Roman proconsul and the capital of the Roman province of Asia Minor. It governed itself as a "free" city through its assembly and senate. In Acts 19:35–40, the city clerk (a leading magistrate) seeks to calm the crowd, for Rome could remove the city's self-governing status if local leaders failed to keep the peace.

Perhaps through the Asiarchs, the clerk already knew about Demetrius' charges. He ridicules the idea that anyone would think Ephesus did not guard the goddess and her temple faithfully. Moreover, he declares that all people know about her special image that fell from heaven—the implication being that it was indeed supernaturally crafted. Finally, the clerk states that the missionaries have not blasphemed Artemis. In so arguing, he dishonors Demetrius but stops short of humiliating him, for he adds that any criminal charges can be admitted following the proper procedures. He implies that Ephesus is a well-ordered city, and the riot endangers that reputation.

A TRANSFORMING VISION

Paul's years in Ephesus reveal the typical pressures he faced and several common results of his gospel message. First, the gospel unleashes the power of God through the work of the Holy Spirit. Those with only the knowledge of John's baptism receive fullness in the Spirit. Those who try to lasso the Spirit's power are overcome themselves by the very forces they try to subdue. Believers are transformed for faithful service as they reject their former pagan ways.

Second, the gospel provokes opposition, which takes several forms. Some Jews are unconvinced by the message that Jesus is the Messiah and seek to distinguish their understanding of Judaism from Paul's group, known as the Way. Some gentiles embrace the gospel message and turn from their reliance on magical arts. Others, like Demetrius, see such transformation as a threat to their livelihood and seek to stomp out the Way.

Finally, some gentiles consider Paul as a client worthy of support because of his interesting ideas, and they declare the missionaries innocent of blasphemy charges. These gentiles save Paul's life, but, ironically, they underestimate the power of the gospel's transforming vision of the individual and society.

Paul eventually faces similar challenges and charges in Jerusalem—accusations that ultimately send him in chains to Rome.

PAUL THE WRITER

SPREADING THE GOSPEL THROUGH EVERYDAY LETTERS

E. RANDOLPH RICHARDS

Reading someone else's mail is usually considered rude, but Christians do it all the time. In fact, pastors encourage it: "Read what Paul wrote to the Colossians." That letter wasn't written to us! Yet as Christians we believe it wasn't just for the folks living in Colossae. God still speaks to us through that old letter.

Because God used everyday letters, the more we know about first-century letter-writing, the better we can understand what Paul was saying to his readers—and what God is saying to us.

We talk about Paul's letter to the Colossians, but the opening line actually reads, "Paul, an apostle of Christ Jesus by the will of God, and Timothy our brother to God's holy people in Colossae."[1] It's common to say that Paul included Timothy as a courtesy, but first-century writers didn't do this; courtesy greetings were included at the end of the letter (see Romans 16:21). Rather, Timothy was a co-sender, which was very rare. God used both Paul and Timothy to communicate his message to Colossae (and to us).

WHEN & WHERE PAUL WROTE HIS LETTERS

We can't be entirely certain about when and where Paul wrote his letters—in part because we're not exactly sure of the timeline for Acts. However, we can assemble a rough chronology based on details in Acts, in Paul's letters, and in archaeological findings. For instance, an inscription found at Delphi, Greece, indicates that Gallio served as proconsul (governor) in AD 51–53—which tells us when Paul first visited Corinth (Acts 18:12–17). The Acts 18 narrative lines up with references in 1 Thessalonians to recent persecution (1:6), Philippi (2:2), Athens (3:1), and Timothy's travels (3:2, 6), supporting the conclusion that Paul wrote 1 Thesslonians after reaching Corinth.

Galatians is perhaps the hardest letter to place on the timeline because the text offers few clues. Many scholars believe Paul wrote it soon after his second visit to Galatian churches; others think it came later, around the same time as Romans, due to similar content in the two letters.

The information below assumes that all 13 letters can be attributed to Paul.

	Paul's location	Date range	Letter
Second journey Acts 15:36–18:22	Troas, Macedonia, or Corinth	AD 48–52	Galatians
	Corinth	AD 50–53	1 Thessalonians 2 Thessalonians
Third journey Acts 18:23–21:14	Ephesus	AD 52–55	1 Corinthians
	Macedonia	AD 53–55	2 Corinthians
	Corinth	AD 55–58	Romans
Captivity Acts 24–28	Imprisoned or confined in Rome (or Caesarea or Ephesus)	AD 58–63	Philemon Colossians Ephesians Philippians
Second period of captivity? (not reported in Acts)	Unknown	AD 64–67	1 Timothy Titus 2 Timothy

THE MORE WE KNOW ABOUT FIRST-CENTURY LETTER-WRITING, THE BETTER WE CAN UNDERSTAND WHAT PAUL WAS SAYING TO HIS READERS—AND WHAT GOD IS SAYING TO US.

A COLLABORATIVE EFFORT

Christians imagine Paul wrote letters like we do today. Whether with pen and paper or with a keyboard, I personally write down my letter. If it is important, I may think about what I want to say, but then I write (or type) as I compose. I might scratch something out, erase, or delete a bit, but that draft is what I am sending. When I am done, I mail it (or email it).

First-century letters were different at every step. But before we get into details about letter-writing, let's consider two fundamental ways we differ from the ancients as people.

Modern Westerners are intensely individualistic. Folks in Paul's day were not. They thought in terms of "we" not "me." Paul did not say to himself, "I need input from my team before I write." Rather, the thought of excluding them never would have occurred to him. He didn't go off to his bedroom to write; it would have been way too dark. He sat out in the airy courtyard. His ministry companions were there; others walked by and listened in, sometimes chiming in their opinions. Discussions and teaching moments likely broke out frequently. Nonetheless, there was never a question about who was the apostle, the one in charge. Like all ancient letter-writers, Paul took responsibility for every word.

In the 21st century, virtually all of us are literate. In the ancient world, probably 20 percent (at most) could read. We speak jointly of reading and writing, but those are actually different skills. In the ancient world, someone who could read quite well would still struggle to scratch out letters. Writing is a matter of practice.

At the end of Galatians, Paul notes, "See what large letters I use as I write to you with my own hand!" (Galatians 6:11). Paul spoke and read at least four languages, but like almost all ancient people, he rarely wrote anything himself. That was secretary's work!

A LONG, THOUGHTFUL PROCESS

What did it look like for Paul to write to the Colossians? He didn't work in a church or home office. He was a man on the road. When he entered a town and began to speak, locals recognized that he was a learned man. Traveling philosophers and teachers were popular, and wealthy people would invite them into their homes. It would not be uncommon for a wealthy person's residential complex to house more than 50 people, including family members, slaves, and employees. Adding a few guests would have been no problem. In Philippi, Lydia invited Paul and his team to stay at her house (Acts 16:14–15).

When hosting a teacher, a wealthy homeowner would usually hold a dinner and invite friends. The traveling teacher would be expected to provide the dinner entertainment, often by reading something he had recently written.[2] For Paul, this likely was a common way to spread the gospel. He was always writing things to share. Some parts of his letters were pieces he had written previously. Paul worked and reworked material as he discussed the gospel with dinner guests, people in the marketplace, and those in the synagogue.

At some point—perhaps during his time in nearby Ephesus—Paul heard of challenges being faced by the church in Colossae. He was not able to travel there in person, so he decided to send a letter. Paul or a colleague went down to the marketplace, to the stalls where the scribes worked. They didn't just sell papyrus—after all, what would the average person do with a roll of papyrus? Scribes were

WAX TABLET

A wax tablet is a tablet made of wood and covered with a layer of wax, functioning as a reusable, portable writing surface.

hired to write letters, and they were paid by the line. A professional scribe provided the entire service of writing a letter: he started by writing rough drafts on wax tablets; once the author approved, the scribe would cut the papyrus, line the sheets, mix the ink, cut the reed pens, and finally write out a polished copy, taking care to use the correct titles and expressions.

We should never imagine Paul dashed off his letters during some quiet afternoon. Each one was carefully composed over weeks, if not months. He would write a section as the secretary scribbled onto a stack of wax tablets. A few days later, the secretary would return with a draft. Paul would hear it, make corrections, and add material. Back and forth the drafts went until Paul was completely satisfied. Then he had the secretary prepare one polished copy on nice papyrus to send.

A WIDESPREAD INFLUENCE

The ancients cared about appearances,[3] and Paul cared for his churches. He wouldn't want to send them a letter hastily scrawled across some rag of papyrus. His letters were too important. They were for public reading (Colossians 4:16). Paul also had a copy made for his notebooks, called "parchments" (2 Timothy 4:13). Letters were sometimes lost in transit, so writers kept their own copies.[4] It's possible that the biblical manuscripts of Paul's letters originated from his personal set.

Most letters in antiquity were the length of 3 John. The average was 87 words. The Greco-Roman world had a couple great letter writers: Cicero and Seneca the Younger (both roughly from Paul's period of history). Cicero averaged 295 words,

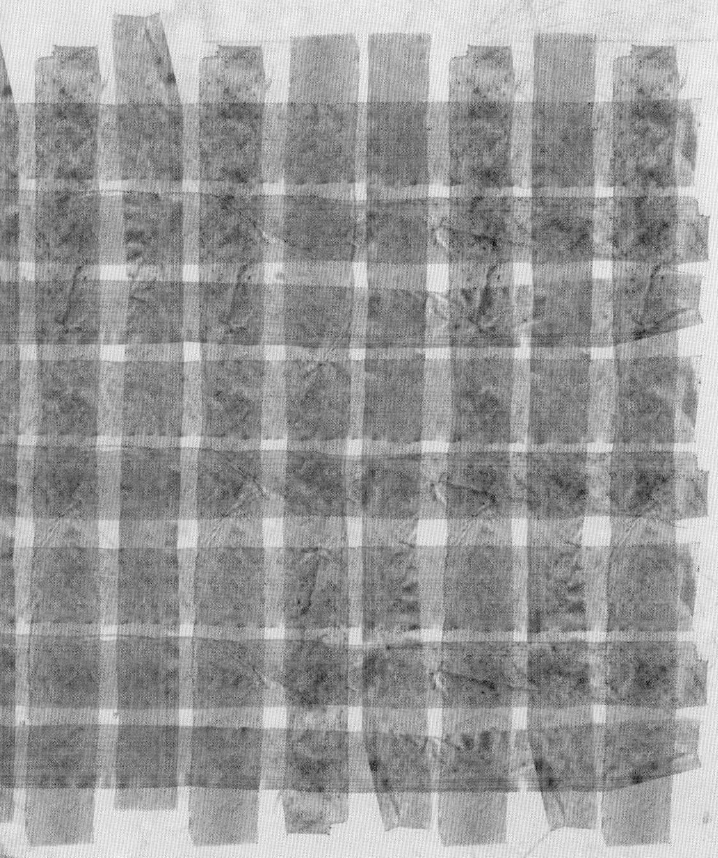

HOW ANCIENT PAPYRUS WAS MADE

To create a sheet of papyrus, the papyrus plant is stripped and smashed flat. The representation at left shows how the strips of papyrus are woven together in layers. Then the sheets are dried and scraped to make a flat surface that's suitable for writing.

Several of the earliest available textual fragments of the New Testament were written on papyrus. Because of this, the term "papyrus" can refer to a class of early manuscripts.

PAPYRUS PLANT

with his longest letter being 2,530 words. Seneca outdid him, averaging 995 words, with his longest at 4,134 words.

And then there was Paul. He averaged 2,495 words, with Romans tipping the scale at 7,114 words! His opponents ridiculed him with a pun: "His letters are weighty and forceful" (2 Corinthians 10:10). When the Christians at Rome received his letter, they must have marveled before they even opened it. Paul had sent them a book, not a letter!

Paul lived in a world where mail flowed constantly. Letters would have seemed like such a minor thing at the time. It's just a letter! Acts doesn't even mention that Paul wrote letters. Yet God chose little things like letters to bring the gospel to the world.

PAPYRUS 46

Many New Testament manuscripts were written on papyrus, a paper-like substance made from the papyrus plant, which is native to the Nile River delta in Egypt. In some cases, full sheets of papyrus have been preserved, but often all we have are fragments. This fragment comes from an ancient papyrus called "P46" and contains the Greek text of 2 Corinthians 11:33–12:9. P46 dates to AD 175–225, making it one of the oldest existing New Testament manuscripts. Although some parts of P46 are missing, the full manuscript would have contained most of Paul's letters.

ΕΝϹΑΡΓΑΝΗΕΧΑΛΑϹΘΗΝΔΙΑΤΟΥΤΕΙΧΟΥϹ
ΚΑΙΕΞΕΦΥΓΟΝΤΑϹΧΕΙΡΑϹΑΥΤΟΥΚΑΥΧΑϹ
ΘΑΙΔΕΙΟΥϹΥΜΦΕΡΟΝΜ[ΕΝ]ΕΛΕΥϹΟΜΑΙΔΕ
ΕΙϹΟΠΤΑϹΙΑϹΚΑΙΑΠΟΚΑΛΥΨΕΙϹΚ̅Υ̅ΟΙΔΑ
ΑΝΘΡΩΠΟΝΕΝΧ̅Ω̅ΠΡΟΕΤΩΝΔΕΚΑΤΕϹϹΑΡΩΝ
ΕΙΤΕΕΝϹΩΜΑΤΙΟΥΚΟΙΔΑΕΙΤΕΕΚΤΟϹΤΟΥϹΩ
ΜΑΤΟϹΟΥΚΟΙΔΑΟΘ̅Ϲ̅ΟΙΔΕΝΑΡΠΑΓΕΝΤΑΤΟΝ
ΤΟΙΟΥΤΟΝΕΩϹΤΡΙΤΟΥΟΥΡΑΝΟΥΚΑΙΟΙΔΑΤΟΝ
ΤΟΙΟΥΤΟΝΑΝΘΡΩΠΟΝΕΙΤΕΕΝϹΩΜΑΤΙΕΙΤΕ
ΧΩΡΙϹΤΟΥϹΩΜΑΤΟϹΟΥΚΟΙΔΑΟΘ̅Ϲ̅ΟΙΔΕΝΟΤΙ
ΗΡΠΑΓΗΕΙϹΤΟΝΠΑΡΑΔΕΙϹΟΝΚΑΙΗΚΟΥϹΕΝ
ΑΡΡΗΤΑΡΗΜΑΤΑΑΟΥΚΕΞΟΝΑΝΘΡΩΠΩΛΑ
ΛΗϹΑΙΥΠΕΡΤΟΥΤΟΙΟΥΤΟΥΚΑΥΧΗϹΟΜΑΙΥΠΕΡ
ΔΕΕΜΑΥΤΟΥΟΥΔΕΝΚΑΥΧΗϹΟΜΑΙΕΙΜΗΕΝΤΑΙϹ
ΑϹΘΕΝΕΙΑΙϹΕΑΝΓΑΡΘΕΛΩΚΑΥΧΗϹΟΜΑΙ
ΟΥΚΕϹΟΜΑΙΑΦΡΩΝΑΛΗΘΕΙΑΝΓΑΡΕΡΩ
ΦΕΙΔΟΜΑΙΔΕΜΗΤΙϹΕΜΕΛΟΓΙϹΗΤΑΙΥΠΕΡ
ΟΒΛΕΠΕΙΜΕΗΑΚΟΥΕΙΤΙΕΞΕΜΟΥΚΑΙΤΗ
ΥΠΕΡΒΟΛΗΤΩΝΑΠΟΚΑΛΥΨΕΩΝΙΝΑΜΗ
ΥΠΕΡΑΙΡΩΜΑΙΕΔΟΘΗΜΟΙϹΚΟΛΟΨΤΗϹΑΡΚΙ
ΑΓΓΕΛΟϹϹΑΤΑΝΑΙΝΑΜΕΚΟΛΑΦΙΖΗΙΝ[Α]
ΥΠΕΡΑΙΡΩΜΑΙΥΠΕΡΤΟΥΤΟΥΤΡΙϹΤ[ΟΝ]
ΠΑΡΕΚΑΛΕϹΑΙΝΑΑΠΟϹΤΗΑΠ[...]
[...]ΚΕΝΜΟΙΑΡΚΕΙϹΟΙΗΧΑΡΙ[Ϲ]
Δ[...]

RUTH ANNE REESE

ACTS 20:1–3

PAUL'S COLLECTION FOR THE JERUSALEM CHURCH

The book of Acts recounts the spread of the good news about Jesus and the growth of the early church. As we follow Paul's missionary journeys, we find many accounts about churches he formed in cities around the Aegean Sea.

Acts 20:1–6 follows directly after the report of a riot in Ephesus. Now that the disturbance has passed, Paul gives some encouraging words to the believers in Ephesus and departs for the Roman province of Macedonia, where he had already sent Timothy and Erastus. Verses 2–5 cover considerable ground and time, encompassing Paul's journey from Ephesus through Macedonia to Achaia (Greece), the three months he spent in Achaia (probably in Corinth), plus the return journey via Macedonia to Troas.

Paul had visited Macedonia during his second missionary journey. There, in the Roman city of Philippi, Lydia became a follower of Jesus and invited Paul to

WITHOUT PAUL'S LETTERS, WE WOULD NOT KNOW ABOUT HIS COLLECTION FOR THE POOR OR THE GENEROUS, SACRIFICIAL GIVING OF THE CHURCHES.

make her home and household his base in the city (Acts 16:11–40). After being jailed in Philippi, Paul faced further persecution in Thessalonica and Berea, but he apparently left fledgling churches in those cities (17:1–15). Acts does not provide many details about these believers, but we do know Paul was drawn to return and encourage them (19:21). To broaden our understanding of his ministry in Macedonia, we can turn to his letters.

A FULLER PICTURE OF THE EARLY CHURCH

The book of Acts and Paul's letters can work together to give us a fuller picture of the early church and its relationship with Jesus. If we had only Acts, we might be tempted to think of the early church in mostly positive terms, without a strong knowledge of the deep spiritual challenges many congregations faced. In Acts, whatever barriers the apostles encounter while spreading the good news are overcome in the power of the Holy Spirit for the glory of God. However, in Paul's letters, we get a different impression of the early church.

Many of Paul's churches were struggling to follow Jesus in the midst of social and economic pressures, and they wrestled with questions about their new faith. These churches raised concerns that Paul answered in his letters. How were new

ROMAN SOLDIERS

Relief fragment depicting the Praetorian Guard (Rome, c. AD 50).

believers to account for those who had died in the faith before the return of Jesus (1 Thessalonians 5)? How were believers to live in marriages with unbelievers (1 Corinthians 7)? Paul's letters and the book of Acts work in tandem to give us a broad understanding of the early Christians and the new life they were receiving in Jesus.

In Paul's letter to the Philippians—the first Macedonian converts—we witness the joy of spiritual friendship as he reports how his imprisonment helped spread the gospel among Roman soldiers (Philippians 1:12–14). Then Paul encourages his friends with news they longed to hear: their friend and coworker, Epaphroditus, was alive and well and was returning to them (2:25–30). Clearly, Philippians is a book of shared joy in the good news of Jesus.

The letter concludes with Paul's gratitude for the gift he received from the Philippians and for their generosity in partnership with him in spreading the good news (Philippians 4:10–18). They were the only church that supported Paul financially, and he indicates that they provided for him more than once (4:16). Even while he was in prison, the Philippians were providing for his needs, leading Paul to describe himself as having more than enough (4:18). Through the gospel, the Philippians had become friends with the one who brought them the good news about Jesus, and they were able to encourage this friend by sharing generously with him.

A CALL TO AID THE POOR

Philippians is not the only place where Paul writes about the generosity of the Macedonians, who struggled with poverty. In 2 Corinthians, Paul uses their sacrificial giving as an example the believers at Corinth should emulate (8:1–4).

Paul's effort to take a collection for the poor is never mentioned in the book of Acts, but his letters indicate that he encouraged the churches of Macedonia and Achaia (as well as Galatia) to give an offering for the impoverished Christians of Jerusalem.[1] During the time when Paul was writing to the Corinthians, a famine was affecting Israel. In addition, the Jerusalem church might have continued to support widows who had no family members to care for their needs (Acts 6:1).

Paul wrote to the Corinthians urging them to set aside money for the collection every week and told them he was going to visit Macedonia on his way to Corinth (1 Corinthians 16:1–5). While in Macedonia, Paul boasted about the Corinthians' readiness for the collection. But since he didn't want to shame himself or the Corinthians, he sent coworkers ahead to make sure the promised offering was ready (2 Corinthians 9:2–5).

Paul urges believers to be generous for four reasons: because Jesus generously gave his life on their behalf (2 Corinthians 8:9); because generosity is a practical way of demonstrating love for one another (8:24); because generosity enables believers to share in God's work and character (9:6–10); and because generosity gives glory to God (9:13).

Accompanied by representatives from the church, Paul ended his third missionary journey by delivering the collection to Jerusalem, to be shared with the poor and to alleviate the needs of the believers there.[2] Without Paul's letters, we would not know about the collection or the generous, sacrificial giving of the churches. Reading the letters together with Acts allows us to see that Paul's visit to Macedonia and Achaia included gathering financial support for the Jerusalem church. Paul hoped to deepen the spiritual bond between the gentile churches and the church in Jerusalem through the sharing of material resources with those in need (Romans 15:27).

Studying Paul's letters guides Christians to rejoice in the spread of the gospel and in the opportunity to give generously to those who labor on God's behalf. Such generosity should cross national and ethnic boundaries to provide for the poor in churches besides one's own. This is a fitting response to God's generous gift to us.

DAMASCUS
ANTIOCH
CYPRUS
PAPHOS
PISIDIAN ANTIOCH
LYSTRA
TROAS
PHILIPPI
THESSALONICA
ATHENS
CORINTH
EPHESUS
MACEDONIA
TROAS

STEPHEN WITMER

ACTS 20:5–12

A LIFE-GIVING MIRACLE

Troas, a major port on the Aegean Sea (on the western coast of modern Turkey), was the city where Paul received his famous vision of a man inviting him to come to Macedonia (Acts 16:6–10). Paul likely founded a church in Troas during his first visit, and he mentions the city in his letters.[1]

The story of another visit to Troas is sandwiched between the tense account of a riot in Ephesus and the tender account of Paul's tearful parting with the Ephesian elders. It also is bracketed by passages providing detailed accounts of Paul's travel schedule, as well as his careful coordination of a sizeable missionary team. The details in Acts 20:1–6 are particularly significant, because they show that Paul's missionary team was with him in Troas when miraculous events occurred. Since Luke himself apparently was a member of the team ("we," Acts 20:6), he was an eyewitness of the events he records.

Although this Troas story is brief, its colorful and miraculous content has made it famous among generations of Bible readers—as well as a sober warning to all who sleep during sermons! Paul stayed seven days in Troas during this visit, but Luke's account focuses solely on one remarkable episode: the death and resuscitation of a boy named Eutychus.[2] In this short passage, covering a single event, what does the eyewitness really want to tell his readers? Based on the details Luke provides, he is telling the story in a way that emphasizes two basic facts: Eutychus really died, and God really raised him back to life.

Acts 20:7–8 sets the scene. Paul and his fellow workers are gathered with the Christians of Troas in an upper room. Here Luke gives us a valuable glimpse of the gathered worship of early Christians: their worship occurs on the first day of the week and includes the breaking of bread. Paul, intending to leave the next day, speaks until midnight, and we're told there are many lamps burning.

Verse 9 describes the tragic accident. The late hour, perhaps combined with the poor air quality of the room (from the smoky lamps), causes Eutychus to fall asleep in his seat at the window. He plummets from the third story and is "taken up dead."[3] Importantly, he's not merely injured, stunned, or momentarily unconscious. He is dead.

In verse 10, attention shifts to Paul's actions, each of which is carefully described. Paul descends to ground level, bends over Eutychus (recalling Elijah in 1 Kings 17:21 and Elisha in 2 Kings 4:34), takes him in his arms, and says to those gathered, "Do not be alarmed, for his life is in him" (note the parallel with Jesus' words in Luke 8:52–53). Paul does not mean that Eutychus is barely clinging to life—we've already been told he's dead—but that God will raise him to life. And that is exactly what happens.

Interestingly, Luke does not describe the moment when Eutychus comes back to life. Instead, Acts 20:11 mentions Paul's return to the third floor, his meal and conversation with the believers (until daybreak), and his departure. Not until verse 12 are we told, "And they took the youth away alive, and were not a little comforted." It seems Luke regards the most important feature to be the results of the miracle—Eutychus' survival and the encouragement it brings to the Christians in Troas.

The way Luke records this short but dramatic episode establishes Paul as God's servant, participating in a miracle on par with the raising of the dead by notable figures such as Elijah, Elisha, Peter, and Jesus himself. But it also communicates something more: the kingdom of God has now come through Jesus and his resurrection, and God's life-giving power is working through Paul as the kingdom advances.

THIS SHORT BUT DRAMATIC EPISODE ESTABLISHES PAUL AS GOD'S SERVANT.

"Paul Raiseth Eutychus to Life," from Figures de la Bible *(1728), by Gerard Hoet and others*

TIMOTHY GOMBIS

ACTS 20:17–38

PAUL'S EMOTIONAL FAREWELL

In Acts 20, Luke records Paul's stop in Miletus to speak with the Ephesian church leaders while on his way to Jerusalem. It is one of the most emotionally powerful passages in Acts, especially the closing scene:

> *When Paul had finished speaking, he knelt down with all of them and prayed. They all wept as they embraced him and kissed him. What grieved them most was his statement that they would never see his face again. Then they accompanied him to the ship.* (Acts 20:36–38)[1]

The opening of the next episode speaks of an intensely painful parting: "After we had torn ourselves away from them, we put out to sea and sailed straight to Kos" (Acts 21:1). What lies behind this passionate farewell?

PAUL KNEW THE EPHESIANS WOULD PROVIDE THE MOST FORMIDABLE OBSTACLE TO HIS MISSION TO VISIT JERUSALEM.

A MAN ON A MISSION

Earlier, Paul had spent three years in Ephesus, so he must have known the Ephesian believers very well (this long visit is covered in Acts 19; see page 90). During this dramatic period of ministry, Paul determined his future travel plans: "After all this had happened, Paul decided to go to Jerusalem, passing through Macedonia and Achaia. 'After I have been there,' he said, 'I must visit Rome also'" (Acts 19:21).

There is a thorny issue of translation here, with some consequences for how we regard Paul's travel intentions. The Greek text lying behind the New International Version's reading of "Paul decided" can be translated more literally, "Paul purposed *in his spirit / by the Spirit* (Greek: *en tō pneumati*) to pass through Macedonia." There is no indication in the Greek text whether this refers to Paul's spirit or the Holy Spirit; it's a matter of interpretation for translators. Did Paul determine his itinerary on his own, or was he directed by God's Spirit? In favor of the Holy Spirit is Paul's later statement to the Ephesian elders: "And now, compelled by the Spirit, I am going to Jerusalem, not knowing what will happen to me there" (Acts 20:22, where the context surrounding *tō pneumati* points to the Holy Spirit).

Luke is portraying Paul on a divine mission to go to Jerusalem and then on to Rome. This closely resembles a feature of Luke's Gospel, where he portrays Jesus on a divine mission to go to Jerusalem. Beginning in Luke 9:51, with Jesus resolutely setting out for Jerusalem, Luke narrates Jesus' journey toward a climactic confrontation (Luke 19:45–46). In the same way, after Paul's resolute statement in Acts 19:21, the rest of the narrative recounts Paul making his way to Jerusalem for a dramatic confrontation (21:17) before heading to Rome (28:16).

FEARING THE WORST

Concern among the churches over what might happen to Paul in Jerusalem is what led to Paul's stop in Miletus to meet with the Ephesian leaders. Paul purposely avoided returning to Ephesus itself and instead arranged to meet the Ephesian leaders in Miletus: "Paul had decided to sail past Ephesus to avoid spending time in the province of Asia, for he was in a hurry to reach Jerusalem, if possible, by the day of Pentecost" (Acts 20:16).

The Ephesians knew Paul better than any other church and they loved him dearly. If they knew of his plans, they would have done anything necessary to prevent him from continuing on to Jerusalem. After all, Paul states in his speech to the elders that in every place he visited the Holy Spirit warned him about what would happen in Jerusalem (Acts 20:22–23).

Luke records several further warnings. After arriving in Tyre, Paul spends a week with the church there. "Through the Spirit they urged Paul not to go on to Jerusalem" (Acts 21:4). It is not that the Spirit is directing Paul *not* to go; rather, the church urgently pleads with Paul to avoid going to Jerusalem after a prophet utters through the Spirit a message about what awaits Paul. In Caesarea, Agabus delivers a dramatic prophetic performance, taking Paul's belt and binding his own hands and feet before giving the Spirit-inspired speech that Paul would be bound in Jerusalem and handed over to the gentiles. The church, including Paul's ministry associates, pleads again with Paul not to go to Jerusalem (21:11–12).

It is most likely the case, then, that Paul intentionally bypassed Ephesus, knowing that the Ephesians would provide the most formidable obstacle to his mission to visit Jerusalem. Had he stopped in Ephesus, he would not have left. Paul was insistent, however, on personally delivering the collection for the Jerusalem church in order to demonstrate the unity of God's one new people in Christ.

A FINAL GOODBYE

In his farewell speech at Miletus, Paul reminds the church leaders of his mode of ministry—how he worked with his own hands to support himself and showed humility toward them. He recalls how he taught them thoroughly and spent himself completely doing so. He also exhorts them regarding the dangers of community breakdown and warns about the threat of evil motives slowly taking root in their hearts, with the risk that some of them might lead people astray.

As Paul speaks, the Ephesian leaders are especially struck by Paul's statement that they would never see his face again. This farewell address, in which he commends them "to God and to the word of his grace," must have stirred their hearts with intense emotion.

Considering the years Paul spent in Ephesus and their dramatic character, it is no wonder he did not want to stop there on his way to his climactic confrontation in Jerusalem. This is what makes the Miletus meeting one of the most emotionally moving scenes in Acts.

Julius Schnorr von Carolsfield, "Paul's Farewell to the Ephesian Elders" (1852), for Die Bibel in Bildern

DAMASCUS
ANTIOCH
CYPRUS
PAPHOS
PISIDIAN ANTIOCH
LYSTRA
TROAS
PHILIPPI
THESSALONICA
ATHENS
CORINTH
EPHESUS
MACEDONIA
TROAS
MILETUS
TYRE & CAESAREA
JERUSALEM

SUSAN WENDEL

ACTS 21:15–36:1–14

THE CHALLENGE OF THE GOSPEL

WHAT DEFINES THE IDENTITY OF GOD'S PEOPLE

When Paul arrives in Jerusalem after his third missionary journey, he faces opposition. Although the elders of the Jerusalem church receive him warmly and glorify God for the success of his mission, they also report the concerns of devout Jewish Christians who have heard that Paul teaches people to abandon the customs defined by the law of Moses (Acts 21:17–26). Later, a different group (Jewish, but not Christian) accuses Paul of profaning the temple and teaching against the law of Moses (21:27–36).

In short, many Jews see Paul's mission to non-Jews (gentiles) as a threat to their distinct ethnic heritage. How does the early Jesus movement respond to this concern?

PAUL'S "APOSTASY"?

Paul returned to Jerusalem during a season of socio-political unrest (around AD 57). Fueled by nationalistic fervor, movements sprang up, in part, to protest Roman infringement on Jewish identity and customs. This volatile situation probably contributed to negative reactions against Paul's mission to non-Jews.

Luke's description of the circumstances echoes an earlier Jewish crisis—the Maccabean revolt (167–160 BC). In the events leading up to the revolt, some Jews had assimilated with Greek culture by removing the marks of their circumcision, forsaking the law of Moses, and thereby committing "apostasy."[1] Conversely, other Jews resisted such pressures by asserting Jewish identity markers and practices: They showed "zeal for the law," had "their children circumcised" despite persecution, and eventually reestablished Jewish worship.[2] Luke describes the

MACCABEAN REVOLT

This engraving in the Macklin Bible depicts Mattathias killing a Jew who was offering a pagan sacrifice, an event recorded in 1 Maccabees 2:23–25.

perceived contrast between Paul and Jewish Christians in a similar way: Jewish Christians are "zealous for the law," but they have heard that Paul teaches "apostasy" from Moses by telling Jews not "to circumcise their children" or to practice Jewish customs (Acts 21:20–21).

Paul's opponents appear to conclude that Paul was behaving like the disloyal Jews who abandoned their heritage and customs during the Maccabean crisis. As Luke goes on to show, however, the Jewish Christians' way of understanding the situation created a false distinction between themselves and Paul.

THE COMMON LIFE AND PRACTICES OF CHRIST-BELIEVERS DID NOT LEAD TO THE ERASURE OF THEIR **DISTINCT IDENTITIES** AS JEWS AND NON-JEWS.

RESISTING A FALSE DICHOTOMY

The Jewish Christians in Jerusalem apparently believed the worst reports about Paul's mission—that he had relinquished his Jewish identity and was teaching others to do the same. Their sentiments belie an either/or attitude: either Paul remains a loyal Jew, or he promotes abandoning the law of Moses. In recognizing these polar extremes as the only two options, these Jewish Christians assumed that unity within the Jesus movement could be achieved only through insisting on absolute uniformity. In Acts 21:22–25, however, James and the elders make two moves that resist the natural tendency to polarize.

First, the Jerusalem elders urge Paul to demonstrate his loyalty to Judaism by joining in a purification rite with other Jewish Christians. Although we cannot be certain about the precise nature of this rite, it probably related to the completion of a Nazirite vow.[3] Whatever its purpose, James and the elders conclude that Paul's participation in this purification rite would demonstrate his fidelity to the law of Moses and appease the apprehensions of his opponents. Moreover, within Luke's narrative, this act by Paul confirms his identity as a faithful Jew who carefully observes the law of Moses.[4]

In addition to advising Paul, the elders make a complementary move that likewise seeks to avoid a polarized community: they reaffirm the apostles' earlier decision of the Jerusalem council to allow non-Jewish believers to retain their distinct identity.[5] The reiteration of the apostles' decree in this context emphasizes that the entire law of Moses should not be imposed on non-Jewish Christians. In other words, non-Jews who believe in Jesus do not have to start living as Jews.

The two-part response of the elders thus shatters the false dichotomy constructed by Paul's opponents. Jews who join the Jesus movement should not abandon their Jewish identity, while non-Jews who believe in Jesus need not become Jews.

EMBRACING UNITY AND DIVERSITY

The prohibitions of Acts 21:25 also served another important function. As some scholars note, these regulations appear to derive from Old Testament instructions for both Jews and non-Jews who lived in the land of Israel.[6] Because of their defiling effects, infractions of these regulations had serious consequences: the violators were to be expelled from God's holy people and land. Accordingly, the prohibitions of verse 25 ensured that Jewish and non-Jewish Christians could live together without violating the sanctity of God's people.

In addition, believers in Jesus shared other important practices, described in Acts 2: repentance, baptism, reception of the Spirit, devotion to the apostles' teaching, the sharing of possessions, table-fellowship, and prayer (2:38–39, 42). Together with these practices, the instructions in Acts 21:25 provided a basis for the early Christians' common life together.

At the same time, the common life and practices of Christ-believers did not lead to the erasure of their distinct identities as Jews and non-Jews. Rather, in the face of nationalistic opposition against Paul and his gentile mission, the Christ-believing community embraced unity alongside diversity. In so doing, they participated in the age-old plan of God for Israel and the nations.[7]

DAMASCUS
ANTIOCH
CYPRUS
PAPHOS
PISIDIAN ANTIOCH
LYSTRA
TROAS
PHILIPPI
THESSALONICA
ATHENS
CORINTH
EPHESUS
MACEDONIA
TROAS
MILETUS
TYRE & CAESAREA
JERUSALEM

ANDREW SUTHERLAND

ACTS 21:37–22:24

RECEIVING THE UNEXPECTEDNESS OF GOD

PAUL'S TESTIMONY SHOWS THE POWER OF HUMBLE FAITH

Arrested in Jerusalem, Paul found himself in the midst of strife that extended far beyond the local riot spurring his arrest. Along with other Jewish Christian leaders of the nascent church, Paul faced a major challenge: being faithful both to his Jewish heritage and to the Messiah whose gospel had unexpectedly opened the way for gentiles to join with Jews as God's people. Though Paul in fact honored both his heritage and the gospel of Jesus, many Jews in Jerusalem did not think so.

In a statement of defense before the crowd, Paul puts the unexpected on display, showing that neither he nor God is who the crowd thinks. Paul's gospel to gentiles in fact comes from within the Jewish faith, from the same God the people are so zealous to follow. By making this argument, Paul challenges the crowd's understanding of God and of themselves.

WHEN GOD APPEARED IN AN UNEXPECTED WAY, PAUL WAS WILLING TO ACCEPT THE ERROR IN HIS FORMER UNDERSTANDING.

PAUL'S UNEXPECTED IDENTITY

Paul's arrest began under false pretenses. He had come to the temple to show that his Christian mission did not reject the Jewish law, but still a mob of Jews accosted him because they believed rumors that he taught disobedience. The riot began when this mob spread the additional rumor that Paul had defiled the temple by bringing in gentiles. The Roman commander (or tribune) then arrested Paul, most likely trying to stop the riot.

Taken inside the soldiers' barracks, Paul asks to speak with the commander, who we later learn is named Claudius Lysias (Acts 23:26). Hearing Paul speak Greek, Lysias mistakes him for "the Egyptian," a political revolutionary the Romans were seeking to capture. Paul's response clarifies his identity: He is not Egyptian but Jewish, and he was born in Tarsus. Since Tarsus was a cultural center for philosophy and literature and a major hub for trade, Paul's remark aims to show he poses no threat to Rome.[1]

With Lysias' permission, Paul steps back outside the barracks and begins his *apologia*—a speech in defense of what one does or believes—to the crowd outside. Speaking in Aramaic, the language of the Jewish people at the time, he gets the crowd's attention.[2] He starts by defending his identity as a faithful Jew: he was born Jewish, raised in Jerusalem, and educated in Jewish laws and customs under Gamaliel (a renowned rabbi). He became zealous to honor God, much like his Jewish audience. Contrary to what the crowd expects, Paul is as faithful a Jew as any.

PAUL'S UNEXPECTED GOD

Paul suggests it is precisely the God of Israel who called him to action. He proceeds to give his testimony of Jesus' appearance on the road to Damascus. As many New Testament scholars have noted, Paul's speech in Acts 22 emphasizes themes important to his Jewish audience.[3] It highlights Ananias' Jewish piety and adds that "the God of our ancestors" chose Paul (22:14). Throughout, Paul is suggesting that the vision that spurred his conversion is not contrary to Jewish faith, but continuous with it.

Perhaps most importantly, Acts 22 includes a second vision of Jesus, who appears to Paul when he is praying in the temple. In this account, Paul resembles Isaiah, who also had a temple vision and was told no one would understand, just as Jesus tells Paul the people will not accept his testimony.[4] Jesus' appearance in the temple suggests he is God; moreover, from the temple Jesus sends Paul "far away to the gentiles" (22:21).

At this point in Paul's speech, the crowd stops listening and resumes shouting. Jews in the first century were not fond of gentiles, and the occupation of their holy city by gentiles (the Romans) only made matters worse. It's understandable, then, why Paul's remarks draw a hostile reaction: not only does he claim Jesus appeared to him in the temple as God appeared to Isaiah; not only does he defend his mission to the gentiles; he suggests his mandate to go to the gentiles came from within the temple of God.[5]

Paul's claim offends the crowd for issues related to ethnic prejudice and the Roman occupation of Jerusalem. But on a deeper level, it offends them because it challenges their foundational understanding of who God is and who they are as God's people. First-century Jews believed Israel was God's chosen nation, and all other nations—the gentiles—could join the people of God only by adopting the Jewish way of life. Although Israel's life before God was meant to be a light to the nations (Isaiah 42:6), Israel had never been sent out on mission to the gentiles or encouraged to accept the gentiles as they are.

When Paul testifies that God sent him on mission to the gentiles, he effectively argues that God's priorities are different from what Jews understood. They had so long prided themselves on being "God's people," but Paul seems to be questioning their claim to that title. Based on what Paul was saying, they could no longer write off gentiles as enemies or identify their own cherished customs as the way of life for God's people. Faced with this unexpected vision of God and of themselves, the crowd revolts.

THE POWER OF THE UNEXPECTED

In both Paul and the Jewish audience, we see the power of theology. How we think about God impacts our understanding of ourselves, others, and our mission.

We also see the power of humble faith. The difference between Paul and his audience is not primarily Jewish religion. Indeed, Paul takes great pains to show his Jewish heritage, and his testimony is presented in distinctly Jewish ways that draw from Jewish scripture. The difference between Paul and the crowd lies in their responses to God's revelation. When God appeared in an unexpected way and with an unexpected mission, Paul was willing to accept the error in his former understanding of God. But when Paul testifies about his new mission, the people in the crowd are unwilling or unable to set aside their own expectations.

Just like these Jews, Paul had great zeal for God—so much that he had persecuted Christians—but his zeal also led him to obey God's call and go to the gentiles. As biblical scholar Darrell Bock explains, this is Paul's defense in a nutshell: "he was where the crowd is now, a persecutor and a faithful Jew; only God's direction has made him otherwise."[6] When given an unexpected vision of the risen Jesus, Paul recognized the unexpected as God. And through this recognition, Paul became perhaps the greatest exponent in the early church for the "gentile breakthrough"—the extension of the gospel to all nations of the world.

As Christians, we too must open ourselves to the possibility that our understanding of God needs correction. Whether we're reading Scripture, listening to sermons, or discussing theology with friends, we always should be seeking God's direction humbly and prayerfully. God will often surprise us. And as Paul's example shows us, when zealous faith meets humility in the face of the unexpected, the Spirit moves powerfully.

HOLLY BEERS

ACTS 22:30–23:11

TESTIFYING ABOUT THE MESSIAH

PAUL BEFORE THE SANHEDRIN

Acts 23 begins a series of trials in which Paul witnesses before the Sanhedrin, Felix, Festus, and Agrippa. This narrative recalls Jesus' trials before the Sanhedrin, Pilate, and Herod. The parallels between Jesus and Paul are intentional, for Luke consistently portrays the disciples walking in the footsteps of Jesus.

Like Jesus, Paul is innocent. But, also like Jesus, his innocence will not deliver him from suffering. In fact, Paul bears witness to Jesus through his suffering as much as through his three famous missionary journeys. This suffering has been the narrative expectation for Paul since Acts 9, when he encountered Jesus on the road to Damascus.

The Jewish Sanhedrin was a high council that advised the chief priest in his dealings with the Roman overlords. Paul calls the council members his "brothers," which may be an attempt to curry favor or an indication that he sees them not as superiors but equals. Paul claims to have a clear conscience, and Ananias' response fits with what is known of him historically. The sources describe Ananias as not priestly in character, but quick-tempered and corrupt; he accepted bribes, participated in theft, and colluded with the Romans.[1]

PAUL IS ANNOUNCING THE REIGN OF A NEW KING.

Paul's response to Ananias is surprising. It is possible that Paul lost his temper and then apologized by quoting Exodus 23:5. He may have had poor eyesight or may not have known the high priest by face, as this was his first visit to Jerusalem in about five years. However, it remains possible that Paul is insulting Ananias, ironically indicating that he did not view Ananias as the high priest because he was not acting like one. Ananias was instead a hypocritical whitewashed wall;[2] in his unjust treatment of Paul, he was disobeying Israel's law (Leviticus 19:15).

Next Paul gives the real reason for his trial and unjust treatment: his hope in the resurrection of the dead. He is not trying to distract the Sanhedrin; resurrection is indeed the crux of the issue. In Acts 23:6, the Greek word translated as "dead" is plural, so the full phrase is "resurrection of the dead persons." Paul is referring to Jesus' resurrection, but he also is pointing beyond that—to the broader Jewish hope of bodily resurrection for *all the faithful*, as part (and proof) of the coming of God's kingdom. Disciples like Paul argue that the Messiah Jesus makes this reality available.

The ensuing argument between the Pharisees and Sadducees (rival groups among the Jewish leaders) is understandable because of what is at stake. The kingdom of God would no doubt initiate a change in the leadership of God's people, dethroning the Sadducees from their place at the top. As Acts 23:8 indicates, the Sadducees did not believe in a future resurrection of God's people, nor did they believe that a person's spirit or angel continued to exist after death while awaiting resurrection. The Pharisees, who *did* believe these things, side with Paul and affirm his innocence (again, recalling Jesus' innocence).

Although Paul avoids judgment here, he will continue to suffer. In this moment of threat, Jesus' appearance and *presence* is part of the encouragement he gives Paul—not a promise of release, but of continuing witness (Acts 23:11). As Paul defends himself in front of religious and political leaders, he is not merely reacting to their accusations. He is proactively testifying to people from across the socio-economic, ethnic, and power spectrums—just as Jesus foretold on the Damascus road (9:15). Paul is announcing the reign of a new king.

Philippe Galle, "Saint Paul in front of the Sanhedrin" (16th century)

PAUL THE CAPTIVE

EVEN IN CHAINS, HE REMAINED CHRIST'S AMBASSADOR

BRIAN M. RAPSKE

When we read about the apostle Paul in the book of Acts, Luke intends for us to remember Paul the captive as much as or even more than Paul the traveling missionary. Luke devotes almost a quarter of Acts to Paul's final arrest and imprisonment—and if you include the account of Paul's troubles in Philippi, the proportion rises to a third!

In Luke's first volume (his Gospel), he describes Jesus prophesying that his followers would be imprisoned for their faithful witness (Luke 21:12). In his second volume (Acts), Luke shows how this was fulfilled by the 12 apostles, by believers generally, and especially by Paul.[1] As Luke explains, Jesus had made it explicitly clear that Paul was given a dual calling—to "carry" Jesus' name before gentiles and Jews *and* to "suffer for" Jesus' name (Acts 9:15–16). Paul's faithful witness would be extensive and painful.

> IMPRISONMENT, FAR FROM BEING AN INTERRUPTION TO OR DISQUALIFICATION FROM MINISTRY, WAS A TRUE EXPRESSION OF IT.

THE GRECO-ROMAN WORLD

As we read about Paul the captive, it's important to consider the ancient Greco-Roman context of Acts.

In Paul's world, people could be taken into custody for several reasons: to protect them from harm; to prevent them from fleeing; to hold them while awaiting their trial, verdict, or execution; or to coerce their participation in a judicial matter. Changes of venue, choked trial calendars, and other difficulties of process could leave defendants in prison for long periods before they got their day in court. In Roman law, imprisonment was not formally recognized as a punishment for free persons, but this potential use was not lost on magistrates.

Defendants were assigned to custody based on legal and social factors—that is, "by reference to the nature of the charge brought, the honorable status, or the great wealth, or the harmlessness, or the rank of the accused."[2] Serious charges generally resulted in a heavier custody; less serious charges, a lighter one. A charge like murder or treason was serious in itself. A lesser charge, however, might be deemed "serious" because of the high status of the victim.

High-status offenders possessing a well-qualified Roman citizenship received better treatment in custody (if they were taken into custody at all); low status and the absence of citizenship resulted in severer forms of custody. From heaviest to lightest, the options were prison, military custody, entrustment to a higher-ranking civilian sponsor, and release on one's own recognizance.[3]

The whole process was vulnerable to corruption through influence, favoritism, and bribery, although there were laws against such practices.

PHILIPPI

Paul's experience in Philippi shows how the system worked. Aggrieved by the financial damage Paul had done by exorcising a slave girl, her owners haul Paul and Silas into court and accuse them of serious criminal activity (Acts 16:16–24).

The apostles are characterized as low-status strangers without merit ("these Jews"). They are accused of subverting the Roman cultural order, disrupting social relations, and undermining the religion that preserved them ("advocating unlawful customs"). Moreover, the accusers call for the court's consideration, as they are citizens ("us Romans").

The apostles are silent.

Superficially, their silence is a puzzle, but it makes good sense. They will not claim the protection of their Roman citizenship when it is being contrasted with their core identity as fulfilled Jews (that is, Christians). To say "we're Roman" would be to deny their loyalty to the Messiah Jesus. Publicly stripped and severely beaten, they are chained and put into stocks in the inner cell of the prison, a place reserved for dangerous, low-class offenders.

Paul and Silas won't trade on their faith, but this doesn't mean they, as Romans, weren't smarting from such vicious and humiliating treatment (Acts 16:35–40). The following day, they stage a sit-down strike, calling for the magistrates to humble themselves, enter the prison, and escort Paul and Silas out for all to see. It is no surprise that the magistrates, alarmed to discover they had mistreated fellow citizens (itself a serious crime), comply fully but implore the apostles to leave.

PAUL THE CAPTIVE – IN HIS OWN WORDS

Pray also for me, that whenever I open my mouth, words may be given me so that I will fearlessly make known the mystery of the gospel, for which I am an ambassador in chains. (Ephesians 6:19–20)

And because of my chains, most of the brothers and sisters have become confident in the Lord and dare all the more to proclaim the gospel without fear. (Philippians 1:14)

For it has been granted to you on behalf of Christ not only to believe in him, but also to suffer for him, since you are going through the same struggle you saw I had, and now hear that I still have. (Philippians 1:29–39)

And pray for us, too, that God may open a door for our message, so that we may proclaim the mystery of Christ for which I am in chains. Pray that I may proclaim it clearly, as I should. (Colossians 4:3–4)

So do not be ashamed of the testimony about our Lord or of me his prisoner. Rather, join with me in suffering for the gospel, by the power of God. (2 Timothy 1:8)

Scripture quotations are from the New International Version.

JERUSALEM

Immediately after Paul's arrest and double-chaining at the Jerusalem temple, the Roman commander (or tribune) presses to discover Paul's status and crime (Acts 21:33–22:29): Is he the Egyptian insurrectionist? Paul replies that he's a Jew and a citizen of Tarsus. But what has he done?

Assuming Paul to be a low-class troublemaker, the commander thinks it's safe to order his interrogation—by flogging. He's wrong. Paul merely *intimates* his Roman citizenship to the centurion in charge, and the proceedings stop. The commander, Lysias, becomes alarmed when he learns that Paul has a more exalted level of citizenship than his own (Paul was a citizen by birth, while Lysias bought his citizenship). Lysias has mistreated his social better. Paul's chains come off and his custody is slackened. He is lodged in the centurions' barracks and permitted to receive a visitor, and his request to the centurion is granted (Acts 23:16–18).

CAESAREA

Like Paul's confinement in Jerusalem, his transfer to Caesarea and two-year stay there demonstrate how custody conditions could be adapted based on status and crime. But this passage carries darker tones as well (Acts 23:23–24:27).

Paul is transferred by a sizeable military contingent to assure his safety. Lysias, concerned about his mistreatment of the prisoner, sends a letter to the governor Felix, manipulating the facts so they redound to his own credit as a defender of all

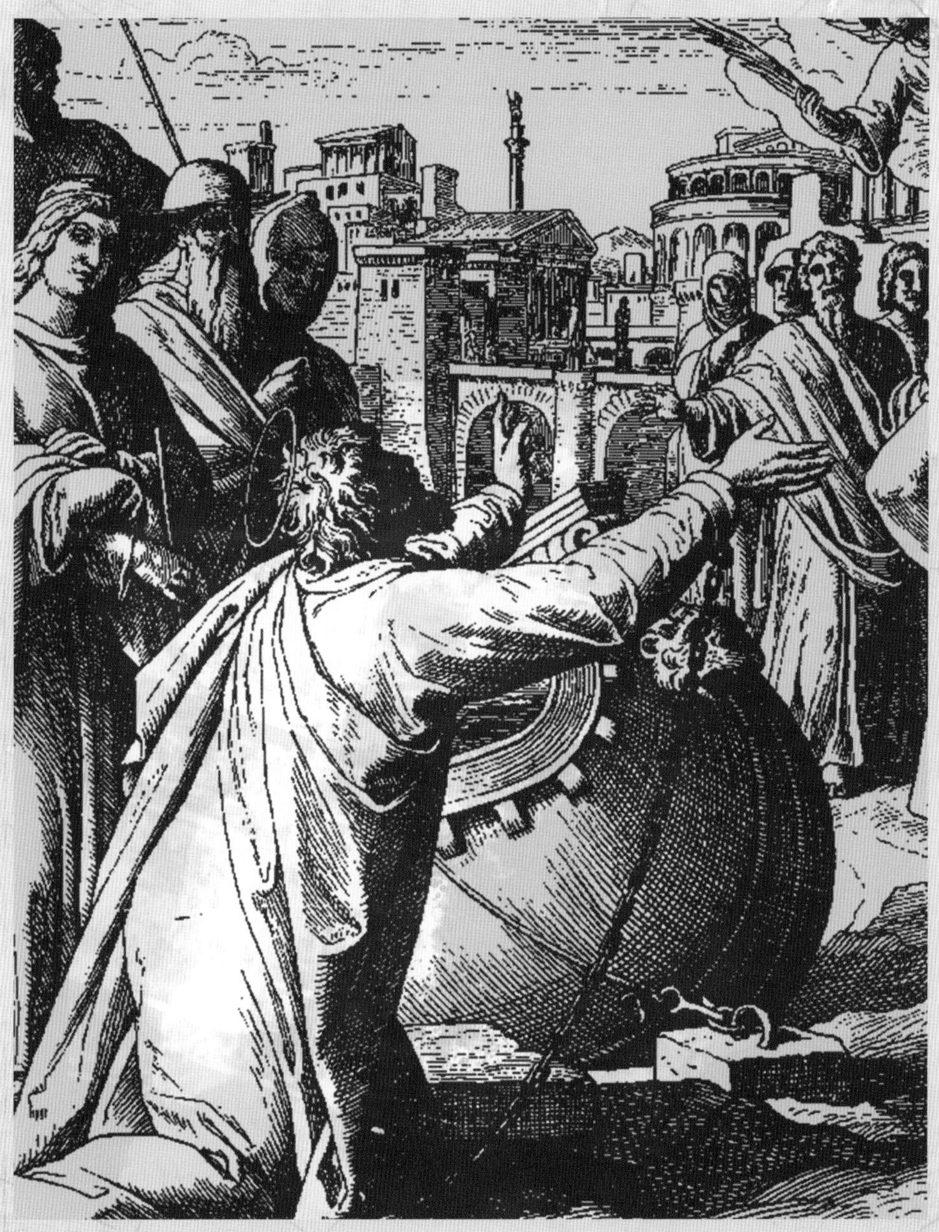

Julius Schnorr von Carolsfeld, "Paul Arrives in Rome" (1860), for Die Bibel in Bildern

things Roman. He writes that Paul's trouble is about matters of Jewish law, but from a Roman perspective "there was no charge against him that deserved death or imprisonment" (23:29).[4] This last point may well have been a help to Paul, intended to heal any bruised feelings he might have about being mistreated.

Felix orders "that Paul be kept under guard in Herod's palace (praetorium)"—that is, in Felix's own official residence (23:35). Later, having heard the Sanhedrin's case and Paul's rebuttal, he adjourns the proceedings, instructing that Paul's military custody be light: "He ordered the centurion to keep Paul under guard but to give him some freedom and permit his friends to take care of his needs" (24:23). Paul likely would have been chained.

Felix's stated resolve to quickly decide Paul's case is empty. In the many days following, Felix speaks with Paul often because he is "hoping that Paul would offer him a bribe" (24:26; perhaps Felix was picking up on Paul's mention of gifts in verse 17). This suggests that one reason for Paul's two-year confinement in Caesarea was his principled resistance to judicial corruption.

Felix leaves Paul in prison as "a favor to the Jews" (24:27). The favor value was that it put an official question mark on Paul's innocence and made him vulnerable to renewed legal action by the Jewish leaders. Eventually, the decision falls to Felix's replacement, Porcius Festus, a magistrate without local experience whom the Jews might be able to influence through charm or pressure. When Festus dangerously suggests a change of trial venue from Caesarea to Jerusalem, Paul cries out, "I appeal to Caesar!" (25:11).

His appeal is granted.

ROME

From Jerusalem to Caesarea to Rome, Paul is a citizen prisoner in the charge of centurions. Once he reaches Rome—where citizenship is common and the social tiers rise well above his own status—Paul is assigned to a single regular soldier to whom he is chained. He is "allowed to live by himself" in rented quarters where he stays "for two whole years."[5]

The rental market in Rome was very expensive, and only the elite few could afford to rent private houses. Paul likely would have rented a room in one of the city's thousands of tenement buildings. Security concerns would have prevented Paul from working at his trade due to the tools involved. As a citizen, he probably qualified for a ration of grain, but the material support of friends would have been critical to his well-being.[6]

Paul's custody in Rome is very relaxed. He is able to welcome "all" (in the tenement's atrium, perhaps) and to preach and teach "boldly and without hindrance" (Acts 28:30–31). Paul's place of confinement seems almost like a house-church. The reason for this remarkably lightened military custody is probably the result of largely exonerating documents from the Jerusalem commander and the governor Festus. Perhaps too there was an oral report from the centurion Julius that Paul never posed a flight risk during the voyage to Rome.[7]

CAPTIVE FOR A HIGHER PURPOSE

On his way to Jerusalem after the third missionary journey, Paul was repeatedly warned by the Holy Spirit that prison and hardship awaited him. He was undaunted: "I consider my life worth nothing to me, if only I may finish the race and complete the task the Lord has given me—the task of testifying to the gospel of God's grace" (Acts 20:23). In Rome, Paul declared to the Jewish leaders, "It is because of the hope of Israel that I am bound with this chain" (28:20). Imprisonment, far from being an interruption to or disqualification from ministry, was a true expression of it.

In his five captivity letters, Paul's conviction that he is a captive for a higher purpose is even more forcefully expressed.[8] He is a prisoner of the Lord Jesus Christ who shares in his Master's afflictions, an ambassador in chains who preaches the unchained word of God.

TIMOTHY GOMBIS

ACTS 23:12–3

THREAT, TRIAL, & VINDICATION

THE CASE AGAINST PAUL DOESN'T HOLD UP

In Acts 23–26, Luke narrates Paul undergoing four trials—one before the Sanhedrin, the Jewish ruling council in Jerusalem, and three before rulers in Caesarea. In an atmosphere of constant threat, Luke portrays Paul as faithful to the scriptures of Israel and driven by the hope of the resurrection of the dead. After each examination, Paul's innocence of any wrongdoing is repeatedly affirmed.

Paul had been arrested because his presence caused an uproar at the temple in Jerusalem (Acts 21:17–36). After another riot nearly broke out at Paul's hearing before the Sanhedrin, the Roman soldiers removed him back to their barracks. It is here that Paul learned of a plot to take his life (23:12–16). Some zealous Jews

PAUL WAS DRIVEN BY HIS FAITH IN GOD'S PROMISES TO RAISE THE DEAD.

had bound themselves by oath to not eat until they had killed Paul, a serious threat that Luke emphasizes by repeating it (Acts 23:14, 21). The plotters sent word to the Sanhedrin regarding their plans and told them to request another examination of Paul. They planned to ambush Paul on his way to the meeting. Paul's nephew learned of the scheme and passed word to Paul, who then relayed the message to the commanding officer, Lysias. This led to Paul's transfer to Caesarea, the seat of Roman authority in the land. To protect Paul, Lysias ordered 470 troops to deliver him to Caesarea in the night.

FELIX

When Paul appeared before the Roman governor Felix in Caesarea, the odds were stacked against him. Ananias, the high priest, came from Jerusalem to bring his accusations. Because Ananias was a shrewd political operator, he brought along a lawyer, Tertullus, in order to help make the case against Paul. One specific charge—that Paul was stirring up unrest— would have made Felix very nervous. Judea was

FELIX

Coin minted in honor of Antonius Felix, the Roman governor of Judea in AD 52–58.

not easily managed, from Rome's point of view, as revolt was always bubbling under the surface. The Romans wanted nothing more than order and control (what they called "peace") in territories they ruled.

Paul made his defense by articulating his commitment to the God of Israel "as a follower of the Way, which they call a sect" (Acts 24:14).[1] On one hand, this was shrewd of Paul, implying the dispute merely involved one sect's interpretation of Israel's religion versus that of another. On the other hand, Paul was being completely forthright, as he considered himself a faithful Jew who was obedient to Israel's scriptures through his proclamation of Jesus as the fulfillment of the nation's hopes. He affirmed that he believed "everything that is in accordance with the Law and that is written in the Prophets," and that he was driven by his faith in God's promises to raise the dead (24:14–15, 21).

This trial ended somewhat inconclusively, as Felix did not really know what to make of Paul and the charges against him. Because he did not see Paul as a threat, he ordered that he be given a comfortable arrangement, where had freedom of movement and could receive his friends.

Paul remained confined in Caesarea for two years. During that time, Felix often entertained Paul and was secretly hoping Paul would bribe him to gain his freedom.

FESTUS AND AGRIPPA

Felix was succeeded by Festus two years later, but the threat to Paul's life remained. The Sanhedrin appealed to Festus to have Paul returned to Jerusalem to stand trial, because "they were preparing an ambush to kill him along the way" (Acts 25:3). When he spoke with Paul, Festus asked if he would be willing to go to Jerusalem to stand trial, but Paul asserted his innocence and invoked his right as a Roman citizen to have a trial before Caesar himself. In a later conversation between Festus and King Agrippa, Festus indicated that the dispute did not involve any wrongdoing on Paul's part, but rather concerned the interpretation of Israel's scriptures and a disagreement over whether Jesus was alive.

Paul's final trial (before he was sent off to Rome) occurred after Agrippa expressed an interest in hearing from the accused apostle. This is Paul's lengthiest defense in Acts 23–26. He stressed that he was a Pharisee and that he regarded this identity as a commitment to the "hope in what God has promised our ancestors" and his faith "that God raises the dead" (26:6, 8). After listening to Paul's long account of his dramatic conversion from persecutor of the church to proclaimer of the resurrected Jesus, Agrippa and Festus remarked to each other that Paul was "not doing anything that deserves death or imprisonment" (26:30).

The narrative of these four trials situates Paul within Luke's overarching purposes in writing Acts. Throughout the book, Luke consistently portrays Christian messengers as challenging the corrupted status quo in places where the gospel advanced, yet they repeatedly are vindicated as being innocent of insurrection. Here, as Luke brings the book toward its conclusion, Paul provides another example of this pattern. He repeatedly demonstrates loyalty to the faith of Israel as an apostle of Jesus Christ and is found innocent by the authorities.

FESTUS

Coin from AD 58/59 minted in honor of Porcius Festus, who succeeded Felix as governor of Judea.

AGRIPPA

Coin minited in honor of King Agrippa II, grandson of Herod the Great. Agrippa II ruled the Jews from AD 53 to 100. His reign was the end of the Herodian dynasty.

JOSEPH R. DODSON

ACTS 27

A TALE OF TWO STORMS

PAUL AND JONAH IN ACTS

Caspian, my 7-year-old, is on the autism spectrum. He obsessively loves to draw. He plows through volumes of blank paper, producing untold numbers of picture books. It is his way of sorting through and making sense of the overwhelming stimuli that flood his little brain.

Today as he was furiously drawing, I asked him what his book was about. Without looking up, he flatly pronounced: "I am making a new Bible." Intrigued, I asked him to let me see a page. He paused the flurry of his pencil to let me take a peek.

At first glance, I saw what was clearly a depiction from Jonah. Sailors were hurling the man of God out of the ship, and a big fish was swimming to engulf the reluctant prophet. But then I noticed two other figures on the stormy sea. I could tell that one of them was Jesus (the halo gave it away), but I had to ask Caspian to identify the other character. Annoyed, he blurted: "That's Peter." I assumed Caspian was confused and had conflated the story of Jonah getting tossed into the sea with the account of Peter walking on the water. Although my son was back to scribbling fiercely on a new page, I couldn't let it go. "Caspian," I said, "Jonah and Peter are two different stories"—to which, unruffled, he replied, "Maybe in *your* Bible."

THE PARALLELS PORTRAY PAUL AS A NEW, FAITHFUL JONAH TAKING THE GOSPEL TO THE NEW NINEVEH.

CONNECTING JONAH AND JESUS

It turns out that my son, rather than being a budding heretic, might not be too far from a biblical reading after all, since New Testament authors also drew from the Jonah story in various ways, such as: (1) making explicit or tacit statements; (2) recalling similar circumstances; and (3) employing key words related to Jonah.[1]

One conspicuous example involves Jesus' references to "the sign of Jonah" (twice in Matthew and once in Luke).[2] Another example occurs when Jesus calms the storm. Readers may recall the events of Jonah 1 when they read about Jesus falling asleep in the bottom of a boat while a storm strikes terror into those around him (Luke 8:23). Just as the sailors wake Jonah to do something—lest "we perish" (Greek: *apolometha*; Jonah 1:6)—so the disciples wake Jesus and shout "we are perishing" (*apollumetha*; Luke 8:24). In the former story, the sea is calmed once Jonah is tossed overboard; in the latter, it is pacified once Jesus rebuffs the waves.

The parallels here probably go beyond the superficial to play a role in deeper narrative dynamics and refined rhetorical maneuvers.[3] For instance, when the seamen ask Jonah who he is, they are filled with fear after the prophet says he worships the God of heaven who made the earth and the seas (Jonah 1:9). Luke likely intends for his readers to remember this response in light of the disciples' question in Luke 8:25: "Who is this? He commands even the winds and the water, and they obey him." The implied answer carried over from Jonah is deafening: Jesus Christ is Lord—over the earth and the seas!

CONNECTING JONAH AND PAUL

With this precedent already set in Luke's Gospel, we should not be surprised to find parallels with Jonah in Luke's second volume, Acts. For example, in Acts 27 a squall hits Paul's ship as he is sailing to Rome. The waves so violently batter the boat that

JONAH IN THE BELLY OF THE FISH

Ancient Christians translated the "big fish" in Jonah as a sea serpent.

Pieter Lastman, "Jonah and the Whale" (1621)

the sailors jettison the cargo and give up all hope of being saved. This alone would probably conjure up images from Jonah in the minds of the original audience.

The similarities between Jonah and Paul, however, highlight their differences more starkly. Unlike Jonah, Paul was not asleep in the boat. Rather, the apostle stood before the panicking sailors and urged them to keep their courage. In contrast to Jonah's glum resignation to be thrown overboard, an attitude that vexes the seamen, Paul's speech invigorates his shipmates as he proclaims:

> *Last night an angel of the God to whom I belong and whom I serve stood beside me and said, "Do not be afraid, Paul. You must stand trial before Caesar; and God has graciously given you the lives of all who sail with you."* (Acts 27:23 NIV)

Moreover, whereas in Jonah the seamen faced the storm because the prophet refused to listen to God, in Acts the sailors run into trouble because they refused to listen to Paul. In Jonah the shipmates are saved because they get rid of the man of God, while in Acts they are saved because they have the apostle in their midst. Jonah refuses to obey God and go to the pagans, but Paul faithfully responds to the Lord's call to share the gospel with the gentiles.

The connections between Jonah and Paul continue when the stories reach dry land. The Lord shows mercy on the people of Malta (Acts 28:1–10) just as he did with the people of Nineveh (Jonah 3). There's even a connection between the fish that swallows Jonah and the serpent that strikes Paul. Catacomb drawings of Jonah demonstrate that ancient Christians translated the "big fish" in Jonah as a sea serpent.[4]

Finally, while the book of Jonah ends with the prophet infuriated about non-Jews receiving the Lord's mercy (Jonah 4), Acts ends with the apostle Paul frustrated because Jews have turned down the gospel (Acts 28:25–28).

A RICH PORTRAIT OF FAITH

The similarities and differences between these stories create moments of suspense, irony, curiosity, and surprise.[5] Their culmination, however, ultimately portrays Paul as a new, faithful Jonah taking the gospel to the new Nineveh (that is, Rome). If Luke writes Acts to be prescriptive as well as descriptive, then one application of these echoes is for us to emulate Paul's resolution to take the gospel to the ends of the earth, in contrast to Jonah's reluctance induced by prejudice, pride, and xenophobia.

To be sure, the Jonah parallels aren't the only ones Luke draws as he narrates Paul's mission. For instance, Luke also seems to be drawing heavily on Homer in the storm narrative (but that's a topic for another book). The idea is not to seek *the* single right allusion of a passage, but rather to embrace the many layers Luke deploys "to reshape the symbolic world in which his readers live and move."[6]

Or more simply put, sometimes we may understand our Bible better through the eyes of an autistic 7-year-old.

JOSHUA W. JIPP

ACTS 28:1–10

STRANDED, SHIPWRECKED, & STILL SHARING THE GOSPEL

PAUL'S FRIENDSHIP WITH HOSPITABLE BARBARIANS

The character portrait of Paul on the island of Malta is of one who benefits the religious and ethnic other, who engages in friendship and meaningful relationships with non-Christians, and who not only extends hospitality *to* non-Christians, but also receives it *from* them.[1] Because Paul is open and flexible, he stumbles into a fruitful opportunity to share the gospel with complete strangers.

SHOWING KINDNESS

In Paul's sea voyage (Acts 27), Luke shows the reader that Paul has a positive relationship with Julius, a Roman centurion. Julius shows "philanthropy to Paul by allowing him to be cared for by his friends" (27:3).[2] Not violent, brutish, or greedy, the centurion embodies the prized virtue of *philanthropia*, Greek for "love of mankind." Later the centurion shows more kindness when he saves Paul's life by disrupting the plan of other soldiers who want to kill all the prisoners after the ship wrecks on Malta (27:43).

Paul's interaction with non-Jewish peoples continues in Acts 28:1–10, which describes another remarkable display of philanthropy and hospitality—this time from the Maltese islanders. Paul is a total stranger to the Maltese, so this is a potentially dangerous situation.

Luke refers to the Maltese as "barbarians" (Acts 28:2, 4). In using this term, he activates widespread cultural assumptions that barbarians would have been inhospitable toward shipwrecked strangers.[3] However, as soon as Luke activates this impending inhospitality scenario, he overturns it—"the barbarians showed

ACTS 27–28 PROVIDE A LASTING IMPRESSION OF PAUL AS ONE WHO WAS OPEN TO FRESH ENCOUNTERS **WITH ALL PEOPLES.**

Gustav Dore, "Paul's Shipwreck" (1843), for La Grande Bible de Tours

us no small philanthropy" (28:2)—describing how the islanders provided a fire to keep the prisoners warm.

Furthermore, according to Greek standards of morality, the natives' kindness to the castaways is the height of virtue, since shipwrecked strangers have no means to reciprocate the hospitality they receive. Once again, the philanthropy of the barbarians toward the needy and vulnerable demonstrates that the Maltese fit alongside other models of hospitality in Luke's writings, such as Zacchaeus, Cornelius, and Lydia.[4]

After Paul's triumphal incident with the viper reveals he is no ordinary prisoner but rather a bearer of God's powerful presence, Publius (the first man of Malta) wisely shows hospitality to Paul and his companions: "He welcomed us and for three days extended friendly hospitality to us" (Acts 28:7). This display of hospitality and friendship elicits Paul's reciprocation of the gifts of the Jesus-like healing of Publius' father and the healing of all the sick on the island. Luke's narration of these healings recalls Jesus' healing of Peter's mother-in-law and his initial healing ministry in Capernaum (Luke 4:40–41). The parallels suggest that Jesus' ministry is continuing to spread to the ends of the earth.

BUILDING RELATIONSHIP

The episode on Malta concludes with the islanders cementing their relationship with Paul: "They bestowed many honors upon us, and when we were about to sail, they put on board all the provisions that we needed" (Acts 28:10). The Maltese "barbarians" are anything but uncivilized. They clearly understand the ways of hospitality toward strangers, for they reflect the attributes of ideal hosts by providing a safe conveyance for the next stage of their guests' journey.

Luke may, in fact, intend for his readers to view the Maltese as beginning a formalized guest-friendship with Paul through their hospitality. When two distinct ethnic parties engaged in a mutual sharing of hospitality, gifts, and friendship, it was often seen as creating a permanent binding relationship—on par with friendship or even non-biological kinship. The Maltese barbarians, then, through their *continued* enactments of hospitality, appear to have initiated a binding kinship-like relationship with Paul.

Paul claims that God's salvation has gone forth to the gentiles who will provide a listening and receptive audience (28:28). The examples of Julius the centurion, the shared meal between Paul and his shipmates, and the hospitable Maltese barbarians provide good reason for the reader to expect that the legacy and mission of Paul will continue even after his imprisonment and death. Philanthropy, shared hospitality, and friendship have been displayed abundantly between these gentile characters and Paul throughout his journey to Rome. Acts 27–28 provide a lasting impression of Paul as one who was open to fresh encounters with all peoples—and a lasting impression of gentiles as receptive, friendly, and hospitable.

CULTIVATING TRUST

Luke portrays Paul not as mocking or demonizing the Maltese, but rather as operating *within* the pagan cultural and religious mindset of the islanders.[5] In fact, he presents these non-Jews as being capable of rightly responding to Paul's message of the risen Christ—even out of their own Greco-Roman cultural and religious traditions. We have already observed three separate occasions when non-Jews show kindness or friendliness to Paul (Acts 27:3; 28:2, 7). In Luke's writings, when a character shares possessions and shows hospitality to strangers, it serves a literary purpose: It symbolically depicts the character's acceptance of God's visitation. It is striking, then, that the Maltese are portrayed as setting worthy examples of both activities—sharing possessions and showing hospitality.

The important point here is that Paul does not demonize the pagan religion and culture of the Maltese. Nor does the narrative present fantastic stereotypes of the islanders, showing them to be superstitious, naïve, fickle, or worthy of being mocked for their inferior rationality. Instead, Luke's Paul is a guest who works *within* his hosts' cultural and religious logic—a logic that enables them to show *philanthropia* to strangers, to recognize God's power working through Paul, to initiate friendship with Paul, and to engage in sharing their possessions.

Clearly, Luke does not valorize Greco-Roman religion; in fact, he presents significant episodes where his characters criticize aspects of Greco-Roman religiosity.[6] He does, however, make abundant use of Greco-Roman religious frameworks in order to show that the early Christian movement meets and even surpasses the highest values of Greco-Roman culture.

In his visit to Malta, Paul—like other believers in Luke's writings—disrupts the expectations of his pagan audience while inviting them to follow Israel's Messiah. And even within their pagan perspective, by God's grace they know how to respond.

CRAIG S. KEENER

ACTS 28:11–31

TO THE EMPIRE & BEYOND

FOR THE GOSPEL MISSION, THE BOOK OF ACTS IS JUST THE BEGINNING

For a long time, Paul had wanted to visit Rome. In Acts 28, he ends up there by means other than those he had originally planned. Now that he is there, however, he continues his mission. Part of that mission is to appear before Caesar's court, but, as always, Paul continues to take every other opportunity to share Christ with everyone he can.

How can Paul carry out this mission under the very nose of the Roman authorities? As Brian Rapske rightly points out, Paul experienced a relatively light custody, as far as Roman custody went (see page 131). He was essentially under house arrest; while he could not go out to visit others, they could come to visit him. Thus, although Paul cannot travel as a missionary, this limitation does not deter him from his mission. All day long, Paul engages his visitors in discussions about Jesus. Even in captivity, Paul remains the missionary that he has been ever since Jesus called him to reach not only his own people but also the gentiles.

PAUL'S PASSION TO SPREAD CHRIST'S MESSAGE IS A MODEL FOR YOU AND ME.

PREACHING AND PASTORING

Paul's ministry in Rome follows a familiar pattern. As in earlier locations, Paul begins with the Jewish community, with whom he shares the most common ground. When some Jews do not accept the message, Paul warns that their rejection fulfills scripture. He explains that their refusal justifies him preaching even to gentiles the kingdom originally promised especially to his own people.

Paul has previously announced his intention to go to the gentiles without really abandoning his own people, and here he announces it again (Acts 28:28).[1] Undoubtedly Paul establishes a foundation—even in the very heart of the empire—of his theological vision for this church. The church must welcome Jews and gentiles on the same terms, and ultimately believers from all peoples united in Christ.[2]

Paul remains not only a missionary reaching new people but a pastor to congregations that he has already founded. Unable to travel, Paul sends letters. Although some scholars believe he wrote these letters from captivity in Caesarea or during a detention in Ephesus that Acts does not mention, Paul's mention of Caesar's household in Philippians 4:22 has convinced a majority of scholars that Paul was writing from Rome.[3] Probably some of the soldiers guarding Paul there, regularly hearing his message, became believers.

Virtually all scholars today recognize that Paul was in custody in Rome when he wrote to the Philippians and to Philemon. Although there is more debate concerning Ephesians and Colossians, we have good reason to believe that Paul wrote these letters at the same time. (Early church fathers agree.)

FINISHING THE STORY

Because the book of Acts ends abruptly, scholars debate what happened after Acts 28. Was Paul ultimately released, executed, or both? Prisoners were not always released after two years without charges, but Acts does suggest that Rome recognized the charges against Paul as being baseless:

- The dossier from Festus and Agrippa surely declared their opinion of Paul's innocence (25:26–27; 26:31–32).
- The centurion who accompanied Paul to Rome may have added his observations (27:43).
- Paul arrived in Rome before any accusers, and even afterward his custody remained light (28:21, 30–31).

Early Christian tradition seems clear that Paul was eventually executed, and Paul may already anticipate such a fate in Acts 20:25 (and 2 Timothy 4:6, 18). But church tradition also suggests he gained his freedom in Rome and eventually preached in Spain.[4] Also, the Pastoral Epistles (1–2 Timothy and Titus) show that Paul worked further in the eastern Mediterranean region, including in Ephesus and Crete.

Tradition further agrees that, when in Rome again, Paul was rearrested and executed during Nero's brutal persecution of Christians there. The idea that Paul was released and later rearrested and executed best fits the full evidence that we have.

FULFILLING THE MISSION

Just as other promises in Acts are fulfilled—such as the coming of the Holy Spirit (1:4–5)—Paul surely fulfilled his calling to reach the nations. Why did Luke decide to end his narrative in Rome? Some suggest it's because Paul was still alive in Rome when Luke was writing—so Luke had simply run out of new material.[5] But his second volume (Acts) is almost the same length as the first (Luke's Gospel), suggesting he carefully designed his narrative to end here, no matter when he finished it.

Whenever Luke writes, then, his narrative might reach its climax in Rome because it is a fitting foretaste of what is to come. The Gospel of Luke begins and ends in Jerusalem; in contrast, the book of Acts begins in Jerusalem and ends in Rome. Christ's commission and promise of empowerment tie these two volumes together (Luke 24:47–49; Acts 1:4–8). Christ's agents must bring the good news about him to all nations, to the ends of the earth.

Acts offers various foretastes of that expectation, describing the apostles preaching to Jews from all nations at Pentecost (Acts 2:5–11), to an African official from what Greeks considered the southern ends of the earth (8:27–39), and now in Rome. Rome was not the "ends of the earth"; indeed, it was the heart of the empire, to which all roads led. But that is precisely the point: If the good news can reach the heart of the empire and thrive there, it can flourish anywhere. Paul preaches in Rome, openly and unhindered; nothing can stop the gospel.

Acts closes not with Paul's death, but with a foretaste of the continuing mission to the nations. We have observed that Paul probably participated in this mission further. More important, this mission to all peoples continues today. Paul's passion to spread Christ's message is a model for you and me. Whatever our respective roles, we remain part of that mission to bring good news about Jesus Christ to the ends of the earth.

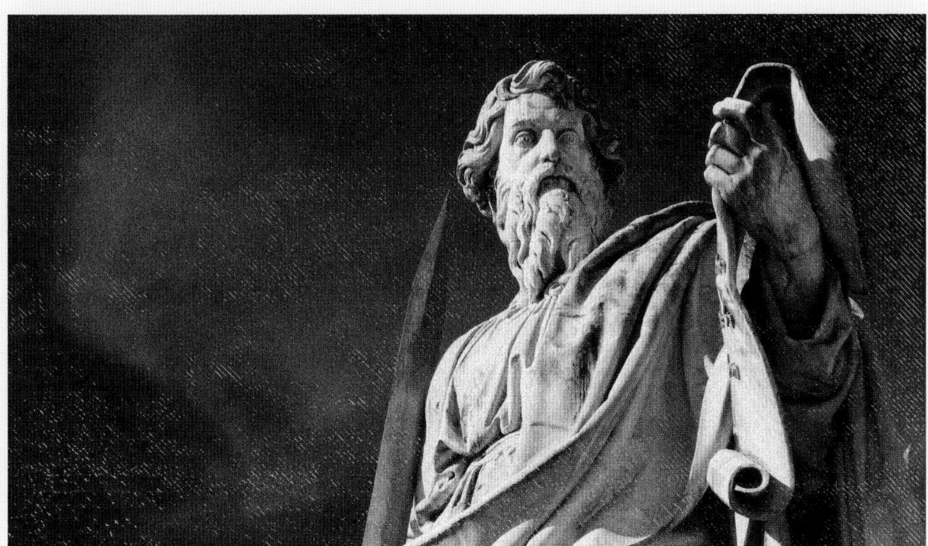

"I HAVE FULLY PROCLAIMED THE GOOD NEWS OF CHRIST"
Paul in Romans 15:19

Statue of Paul in Vatican City, Rome

NOTES

THE JOURNEY TO DAMASCUS

WHO WERE THE PHARISEES?

[1] It's likely that the Pharisees developed into the rabbinic movement in the second century. However, since rabbinic sources are influenced by the two Jewish revolts against Rome and subsequent events, they are difficult to use for understanding the Pharisees in the first century.

[2] Josephus, *Jewish Antiquities* 15.370, 17.41–42, 18.12.

[3] Josephus, *Jewish Antiquities* 18.4, *Jewish War* 1.648–651.

[4] For more on the Pharisees, two good starting places are: Lynn Cohick, "Pharisees," in *Dictionary of Jesus and the Gospels* (IVP, 2013), 673–79; and the chapter on the Pharisees in William A. Simmons, *Peoples of the New Testament World* (Hendrickson, 2008).

WHO WERE THE CHRISTIANS SAUL PERSECUTED?

[1] The letter of James gives us a sense of his teachings. According to the early church historian Eusebius, James' nickname was "James the Just," and his knees were hard like a camel's because he prayed so often in the temple (*Ecclesiastical History* 2.23.6–7).

[2] For examples of these activities, see Acts 2:14–36; 12:5, 12; 16:25; 20:7–11; 1 Cor 14; Eph 5:19; 6:18; Col 3:16; Heb 1–10; Jas 5:13–14; Jude 20. Women were vocal participants in all these activities; see Acts 16:15, 40; 18:26; Rom 16:1–16; 1 Cor 11:5; Phil 4:2–3.

[3] On hospitality, note Acts 11:1–3; Gal 2:12; also see Acts 2:46; 1 Cor 10:16–17, 11:20–22; Jude 12. For examples on sharing each other's burdens, see Acts 6:1; 11:27–30; Heb 13:16; also see Acts 2:44; 4:32; Rom 12:13; 2 Cor 8–9; Jas 2:15–16; 1 John 3:17.

A NEW HOPE AND DIVINE DIRECTION

[1] For a comprehensive treatment on divine oracles, see James R. McConnell, *The Topos of Divine Testimony in Luke–Acts* (Eugene, OR: Pickwick, 2014).

[2] Plato, *Apology* 20e–21d.

[3] Luke sets the precedent for this in his Gospel, which begins with vague oracles about Jesus and John. For instance, Simeon foretells how Mary will suffer as her son grows up to cause the rise and fall of many in Israel (Luke 2:34–35), and the angel informs Zechariah that his son will lead many from Israel back to their God (1:16–17). Luke even begins Acts with a prophetic oracle that becomes the overarching thesis and outline for the book: "You will receive power when the Holy Spirit comes on you; and you will be my witnesses in Jerusalem, and in all Judea and Samaria, and to the ends of the earth" (Acts 1:8). Readers should expect God to speak throughout Acts even after Jesus has ascended to heaven. This is underlined by Peter's first sermon to the Pentecost crowd declaring that their sons and daughters will prophesy, their young and old will see visions and dreams, and the Lord will display wonders in the heavens above (2:17–19).

[4] Paul's first message from the Lord is so crucial Luke includes it three times in Acts (9:3–6; 22:6–10; 26:13–16). In Acts 26, Paul adds that the Lord also said to him during the encounter: "I will rescue you from your own people and from the Gentiles. I am sending you to them to open their eyes and turn them from darkness to light, and from the power of Satan to God, so that they may receive forgiveness of sins and a place among those who are sanctified by faith in me" (26:17–18).

[5] Scripture quotations are from the New International Version.

[6] Regarding how the order here (gentiles, kings, and Israel) relates to Paul's preaching pattern in Acts (Jews, gentiles, and kings), see Beverly Roberts Gaventa, *Acts* (Nashville: Abingdon, 2003), 152.

TRANSFORMED BY THE MESSIAH

[1] For this article I have borrowed substantially from the relevant portion of my recent book *The Righteous & Merciful Judge: The Day of the Lord in the Life and Theology of Paul* (Bellingham: Lexham Press, 2018), 77–93.

[2] Scripture quotations are from the New English Translation.

[3] See Jeffrey W. Aernie, *Is Paul Also Among the Prophets? An Examination of the Relationship between Paul and the Old Testament Prophetic Tradition in 2 Corinthians,* LNTS 467 (London: T&T Clark, 2012); Tony Costa, "Is Saul of Tarsus

Also Among the Prophets? Paul's Calling as Prophetic Divine Commissioning" in *Christian Origins and Hellenistic Judaism: Social and Literary Contexts for the New Testament,* ed. Stanley E. Porter and Andrew W. Pitts, vol. 2 of Early Christianity in its Hellenistic Context, ed. Stanley E. Porter and Wendy J. Porter (Leiden: Brill, 2013); Karl Olav Sandnes, *Paul –One of the Prophets? A Contribution to the Apostle's Self-Understanding,* WUZNT 43 (Tübingen: Mohr/Siebeck, 1991).

[4] On theophany, see Exod 3–4; Isa 6:1; Ezek 1:26–28; compare Acts 9:3; 22:6; 26:13; 1 Cor 9:1; Gal 1:16a.

On unworthiness, see Exod 4:10; Isa 6:5; Jer 1:6; Ezek 1:28; compare 1 Cor 15:9; 2 Cor 2:16, 3:5.

On the Lord's enabling, see Isa 6:6–7; Jer 1:7–8; compare 2 Cor 12:10.

On the giving of a divine message, see Exod 4:12; Jer 1:9–10; Ezek 2:4; compare 1 Cor 15:1–3; Gal 1:11–12.

On authority, see Exod 4:1–17; Isa 6:8–9; Jer 1:10; Ezek 2:3; compare 2 Cor 10:8, 17; 3:10.

These five elements were adopted from Scott J. Hafemann, *Paul, Moses, and The History of Israel* (Eugene, OR: Wipf & Stock, 2008), 50–59; John B. Polhill, *Paul and His Letters* (Nashville: B&H Academic, 1999), 50–51. See also Craig A. Evans, "Prophet, Paul as," *Dictionary of Paul and His Letters,* 762–65.

[5] 2 Corinthians 3:5; 4:7–18. For more on this theme, see Paul Barnett, *The Second Epistle to the Corinthians,* NICNT (Grand Rapids: Eerdmans, 1997), 173; Aernie, *Is Paul Also Among the Prophets?,* 118–19; Timothy B. Savage, *Power Through Weakness: Paul's Understanding of the Christian Ministry in 2 Corinthians,* SNTSMS 86 (Cambridge: Cambridge University Press, 1996).

THE FIRST MISSIONARY JOURNEY AND THE JERUSALEM COUNCIL

ANTIOCH: PAUL'S GATEWAY TO THE WEST

[1] Frederick Norris, "Antioch (Place) (Antioch of Syria)," *Anchor Bible Dictionary*, 1:265–67.

[2] Rodney Stark, *Cities of God*, (HarperOne: New York, 2007).

[3] This is evident from Acts 12:25–13:3; 14:26; 18:22.

[4] "Hellenist" was a label for a Greek-speaking Jew. However, the editors of the United Bible Society Greek New Testament admit difficulty in determining between "Hellenists" and "Greeks," both of which have significant textual support. The "Hellenists" likely included gentiles.

[5] Norris, "Antioch," 266.

PISIDIAN ANTIOCH: THE GOOD NEWS OF SALVATION

[1] Scripture quotations are from the English Standard Version.

[2] For examples, see Gal 6:14; 1 Cor 1–2, 15.

LYSTRA: A VISIT FROM THE GODS?

[1] Allusions also could be used to demonstrate erudition or to establish a link with the audience by appealing to a shared knowledge. For more reasons, see Benjamin D. Sommer, *A Prophet Reads Scripture: Allusion in Isaiah 40–66* (Stanford: Stanford University Press, 1998), 19. See also E. Randolph Richards, Richard S. Hess, Joseph R. Dodson, et. al, *Read Scripture Deeply: An Introduction to Intertextuality* (Fort Worth, TX: IBR, 2015).

[2] Sommer, *A Prophet Reads Scripture*, 19.

[3] Scripture quotations are from the New Revised Standard Version.

[4] See Acts 17:18. Also see C. Kavin Rowe, *World Upside Down: Reading Acts in the Graeco-Roman Age* (Oxford: Oxford University Press, 2010), 27–41.

[5] For more on this, see Osvaldo Padilla, *The Acts of the Apostles: Interpretation, History and Theology* (London: Apollos, 2016), 177–84.

[6] Translations vary, but "uneducated babbler" captures the gist of the philosophers' insult in Acts 17:18 (the Greek word is *spermologos*). On the converts at Athens, see Acts 17:34.

[7] Ovid, *Metamorphoses*, Book VIII, lines 679–724 (the transformation of Philemon and Baucis).

PAUL THE MISSIONARY: PREACHING TO EVERYONE, EVERYWHERE

[1] Scripture references are from the New International Version. Paul's whereabouts during this period are described in Acts 9:19–30; 11:25–26; Gal 1:15–24.

[2] For examples of these methods, see Acts 9:20–22; 13:5, 15–41, 46–49; 14:1, 8–11; 17:2–4, 10–12, 17; 18:4–5; 19:8; 20:20.

[3] Paul's response to rejection can be seen, for example, in Acts 13:45–48; 14:5–7, 19–20.

[4] See Acts 14:21, 25. Note that most English Bibles use the spelling "Perga"—an idiosyncratic transcription of the Greek that classical scholars do not use.

[5] Stephen Mitchell, *Anatolia: Land, Men, and Gods in Asia Minor* (Oxford University Press, 1993), 2:7.

THE JERUSALEM COUNCIL: THE GOOD NEWS CROSSES ETHNIC BORDERS

[1] Acts 10:20; see also Gal 2:11–12.

[2] See Gal 2:19; 3:14.

[3] Gal 1:8–9. Scholars disagree as to whether Paul wrote his letter to the Galatians before or after the council in Jerusalem. Since the letter does not appeal to the ruling, it makes good sense that he wrote it before the council. The ruling would have been a powerful argument for Paul and would have silenced his opponents in Galatia, since they held the Jerusalem church leaders in high esteem.

[4] Scripture quotations are from the New Revised Standard Version.

THE SECOND MISSIONARY JOURNEY

THE UNSTOPPABLE GOSPEL

[1] These circumstances are apparent from Acts 15:36–41; 16:3–4; 16:6–10.

PAUL THE TRAVELER: A DAY'S JOURNEY WITH PAUL

[1] These estimates of distances and travel time come from Orbis, a mapping system for the ancient Roman Empire (orbis.stanford.edu).

[2] Acts 15:41; 16:6–12; 17:1, 10, 14–15; 18:18–22.

[3] Sources include Horace, *Satires* 1.5 and *Epistles* 1.52–61; Valerius Maximus, *Memorable Deeds* 1.7, ext. 10; Seneca the Younger, *Beneficiis* 4.17.4, 4.37.1–2, *Brevitate Vitae* 9.5, and *Epistles* 96.4, 107.2; Quintilian, *Institutes* 4.5.23; Pliny the Elder, *Natural History* 9.154; Pliny the Younger, *Epistles* 6.25, 8.1, 10.15–17; and Plutarch, *Table-Talk* 2.643D, 8.721D. See also Lawrence Keppie, *Understanding Roman Inscriptions* (Baltimore: Johns Hopkins University Press, 1991), 60–69; and Jo-Ann Shelton, *As the Romans Did: A Sourcebook in Roman Social History* (Oxford University Press, 1998), pages 323–28.

[4] Note Rom 15:30–32; 2 Cor 1:10–11; Phlm 22.

[5] As in Rom 12:13; Heb 13:2.

[6] See Acts 16:15; 17:5; 18:3.

TROAS & PHILIPPI: WHO'S CALLING?

[1] The sense that Paul envisioned a "certain" man from Macedonia is conveyed by the word *tis* in the Greek text: *anēr Makedōn tis*.

[2] In comparison, "the man from Mount Vernon" might elicit in the minds of Americans the impression of George Washington.

[3] The man in Alexander's vision was a Jewish high priest; see Josephus, *Jewish Antiquities* 11.333–35 and Pseudo-Callisthenes *Life of Alexander of Macedon* 1:35; compare Suetonius *Julius* 32.

[4] Ben Witherington III, *The Acts of the Apostles: A Social-Rhetorical Commentary* (Grand Rapids: Eerdmans, 1998), 480. For Paul, of course, the mission involved a significantly different kingdom.

[5] There has been a rise of biblical scholars applying these ideas to the Gospels to help us understand them better. For example, see the survey in Karl McDaniel, *Experiencing Irony in the First Gospel: Suspense, Surprise, and Curiosity* (LNTS; London: Bloomsbury, 2013), 1–41.

[6] Literally: *"obscurcissement stratégique."* Raphael Baroni, *La tension narrative : suspense, curiosité et surprise* (Paris: Seuil, 2007), 124.

[7] Meir Sternberg, "Universals of Narratives and their Cognitivist Fortunes (I)," *Poetics Today* 24, no. 2 (2003): 297–395.

[8] See Witherington, *The Acts of the Apostles,: A Social-Rhetorical Commentary* (Grand Rapids: Eerdmans, 1998), 487.

[9] See Robert C. Tannehill, *The Narrative Unity of Luke-Acts* (vol. 2; Minneapolis: Fortress, 1994), 196.

PHILIPPI: DEFAMED AND VINDICATED IN A ROMAN COLONY

[1] Scripture quotations are from the New International Version.

[2] See Phil 1:29; Col 1:24; 2 Tim 2:3.

[3] See 1 Cor 9:1–18.

THESSALONICA: TURNING THE WORLD UPSIDE DOWN

[1] See Acts 22:3–5; Phil 3:6.

[2] See Acts 19:27; 1 Pet 2:11–17; Tacitus, *Histories* 15.44; Suetonius, *Nero* 16; and Pliny the Younger, *Epistle* 10.96.

[3] Note Luke 14:25–33; 22:24–27; Acts 16:25–34; 17:22–31; 20:17–35.

[4] Craig S. Keener, *Acts: An Exegetical Commentary* (Grand Rapids: Baker Academic, 2014), vol. 3, 2545–46.

[5] See Acts 17:9–10, 14; compare Luke 23:1–5, 13–16.

[6] See 1 Thess 1:6–10.

ATHENS: PREACHING CHRIST IN A PLACE WITH MANY GODS

[1] Darrell L. Bock, *Acts* (Baker Academic, 2007), 563.

[2] William H. Willimon, *Acts* (Westminster John Knox Press, 2010), 142–43.

CORINTH: PAUL'S BOOMTOWN

[1] Strabo, *Geography* 8.2.23.

[2] S.J. Hafemann, "Corinthians, Letters to the," in the *Dictionary of Paul and his Letters*, ed. Gerald F. Hawthorne, et al. (Downer's Grove, IL: IVP Academic, 1993), 173.

[3] Hafemann, "Corinthians," 174–75.

[4] For example, see 1 Cor 12–13.

PAUL THE PASTOR: CULTIVATING FAITH, NURTURING THE CHURCH

[1] Scripture quotations are the author's translation.

[2] On Timothy's arrival, see 1 Thess 3:6. On Paul's use of coworkers, see 1 Cor 4:17; 16:10–12; 2 Cor 2:12–13; 7:5–16; Phil 2:19–30.

[3] See 1 Cor 11:23; 15:1–3.

[4] 1 Cor 16:5–9; 2 Cor 12:14; 13:1; Phil 2:19, 24; 1 Thess 2:17–18; 3:11.

[5] 1 Cor 1:8; Gal 4:11; Phil 2:15–16; 1 Thess 3:13.

THE THIRD MISSIONARY JOURNEY

PAUL'S TRAVEL COMPANIONS ON THE THIRD JOURNEY

[1] 1 Cor 16:3–4; 2 Cor 9:4.

[2] For examples of Timothy's service to Paul, see 1 Cor 4:17; 16:10; 2 Cor 1:19; Phil 2:19; 1 Thess 3:2, 6.

PRESSING ON WITH THE MISSION

[1] 1 Cor 16:5–8; 2 Cor 1:8; 2:12–13; 7:5; Rom 15:25–26; 16:23.

[2] 1 Cor 16:1–4; 2 Cor 8:1–9:5; Rom 15:25–28.

PAUL THE WRITER: SPREADING THE GOSPEL THROUGH EVERYDAY LETTERS

[1] Scripture quotations are the author's translation.

[2] Cicero, *Epistulae ad Familiares* 16.10.2

[3] Cicero, *Epistulae ad Atticum* 13.14–25

[4] Cicero, *Epistulae ad Familiares* 9.26.1

MACEDONIA AND ACHAIA: PAUL'S COLLECTION FOR THE JERUSALEM CHURCH

[1] 1 Cor 16:1; Rom 15:26; 2 Cor 8–9.

[2] Rom 15:25; 1 Cor 16:3–4; 2 Cor 8:13–14.

TROAS: A LIFE-GIVING MIRACLE

[1] 2 Cor 2:12; 2 Tim 4:13.

[2] The Greek term used to describe him, *neanias*, also can refer to a young man.

[3] Scripture quotations are from the English Standard Version.

MILETUS: PAUL'S EMOTIONAL FAREWELL

[1] Scripture quotations are from the New International Version.

THE JOURNEY TO ROME

JERUSALEM: THE CHALLENGE OF THE GOSPEL

[1] The Maccabean revolt is recorded in 1 Maccabees, a book not included in many Protestant versions of the Bible. On the origins of the revolt, see 1 Macc 1:14–15, 48; 2:15, 46.

[2] 1 Macc 2:23–27; 1:60–61; 4:36–58.

[3] The similarity to a Nazarite vow is based on the reference to head-shaving (see Num 6:1–21, especially v. 18).

[4] See also Acts 16:3; 18:18; 23:3, 6; 24:14–18; 26:4–8; 28:17–20.

[5] For the initial decision, see Acts 15:19–20, 28–29; also see page 50.

[6] For example, Lev 17:8–18:30.
[7] Isa 2:1–4.

JERUSALEM: RECEIVING THE UNEXPECTEDNESS OF GOD

[1] Darrell L. Bock, *Acts* (Baker Academic, 2007), 657.
[2] The Greek text of Acts 21:40 and 22:2 uses the word *hebrais,* which in the New Testament can refer to Hebrew or Aramaic. Aramaic is more likely here, since it was the dominant spoken language at the time. Paul's use of Aramaic demonstrates to those present that he is a Jew and respects their culture.
[3] For example, Luke Timothy Johnson, *The Acts of the Apostles* (Liturgical Press, 2005), 394.
[4] Compare Isa 6:1, 8–10 and Acts 22:18, 21.
[5] Justo González, Acts: *The Gospel of the Spirit* (Orbis Books, 2001), 249.
[6] Bock, *Acts*, 663.

JERUSALEM: TESTIFYING ABOUT THE MESSIAH

[1] Josephus, *Jewish Antiquities*, 20.205–207, 209, 213; Babylonian Talmud, Tractate Pesahim 57a.
[2] Ezek 13:10–12; compare Jesus' critique of the Pharisees in Matt 23:27.

PAUL THE CAPTIVE: EVEN IN CHAINS, HE REMAINED CHRIST'S AMBASSADOR

[1] On the 12 apostles, see Acts 4:3; 5:18–25; 12:1–19; on believers generally, see 8:3; 9:2, 14; 22:4–5; 26:10; on Paul, see 16:16–40; 20:23; 21:11–13; 21:27–28:31).
[2] The Roman jurist Ulpian in Justinian, *Digest* 48.3.1, ed. T. Mommsen, P. Krueger, and A. Watson, 4 vols. (Philadelphia: University of Pennsylvania Press, 1985).
[3] *Digest* 48.3.1.
[4] Scripture quotations are from the New International Version.
[5] Acts 28:16, 20, 23, 30.
[6] Phil 2:25, 29–30; 4:10–20; see also 2 Tim 1:16–18.
[7] On the documents from Lysias and Festus, see Acts 23:29; 25:25–27; 26:32; on the possibility of a report from Julius, see 27:1, 3, 43.
[8] Eph 3:1; 4:1; 6:19–20; Phil 1:29–30; Col 1:24; 2 Tim 1:8; 2:8–9; Phlm 1, 9–10.

CAESAREA: THREAT, TRIAL, AND VINDICATION

[1] Scripture quotations are from the New International Version.

MEDITERRANEAN SEA: A TALE OF TWO STORMS

[1] See Dale C. Allison, *The New Moses: A Matthean Typology* (Minneapolis: Fortress Press, 1993), 19–20.
[2] Matt 12:38–41; 16:1–4; Luke 11:29–30.
[3] See Christopher L. Redmon, "Faithless Israel, Faithful Gentiles: Ethnic Irony in Jonah and Matthew" (honors thesis supervised by Joseph R. Dodson; Ouachita Baptist University, Arkadelphia, AR, April 2014), 1–30.
[4] The comparisons between Jonah and Paul arguably go all the way back to the apostle's calling in Acts 9. Luke might intend for the reader, in retrospect, to see a pun between the homophones in Paul's hometown of "Tarsus" and Jonah's flight to "Tarshish"—especially since another famous ancient historian even identified Tarshish as the Tarsus of Cilicia (Josephus, *Antiquities* 1.6.1). For more on these connections, see Collin Battaglia, "Exploring Paul as the Anti-Jonah in Acts" (honors thesis supervised by Joseph R. Dodson, Ouachita Baptist University, Arkadelphia, Arkansas; April 2017), 1–35.
[5] See Karl McDaniel, *Experiencing Irony in the First Gospel: Suspense, Surprise, and Curiosity* (London: Bloomsbury, 2013).
[6] Richard B. Hays, "Apocalyptic Poiesis in Galatians" in *Galatians and Christian Theology* (ed. M.W. Elliott et al.; Grand Rapids: Baker, 2014), 205.

MALTA: STRANDED, SHIPWRECKED, AND STILL SHARING THE GOSPEL

[1] I have adapted a portion of my argument in Joshua W. Jipp, "Philanthropy, Hospitality, and Friendship," *Christian Reflection* (2015): 65–72.
[2] Scripture quotations are the author's translation.
[3] For example, when the Greek hero Odysseus encountered a new land and people in his voyages, he often spoke the phrase: "Alas, to the land of what mortals have I now come? Are they insolent, wild, and unjust? Or are they hospitable to strangers and fear the gods in their thoughts?" (Homer, *Odyssey* 6.119–121).

[4] See Luke 19:1–10; Acts 10:1–11:18; 16:11–15.

[5] This paragraph is adapted from Joshua W. Jipp, "Hospitable Barbarians: Luke's Ethnic Reasoning in Acts 28:1–10," *Journal of Theological Studies* 68 (2017): 23–45.

[6] For examples, see Acts 12:20–23; 14:8–18; 19:8–40.

ROME: TO THE EMPIRE AND BEYOND

[1] For Paul's earlier statements, see 13:46–47; 18:6.

[2] Rom 1:16–17; 3:9, 29; 9:24; 10:12; 11:25–32; 15:7–13.

[3] Caesar's "household" was not just his family but his staff and servants, including members of his praetorian guard. On Caesarea, see Acts 23:33–35; for hints of an Ephesus imprisonment, see Rom 16:7; 1 Cor 15:32; 2 Cor 1:8–10.

[4] On Paul's desire to visit Spain, see Rom 15:24, 28. For church tradition on Paul's fate, see *1 Clement* 5.5–7; Eusebius, *Ecclesiastical History*, 2.22.1–7.

[5] For the view that Luke wrote Acts while Paul was still living, see F.F. Bruce, *The Acts of the Apostles,* 1st ed. (Grand Rapids: Eerdmans, 1951), 11, 481. However, Bruce changed his mind in favor of a later date for Acts in his final edition, *The Acts of the Apostles*, 3rd rev. and enl. ed. (Grand Rapids: Eerdmans, 1990), 16–17.

IMAGE CREDITS

All images public domain unless otherwise noted.

p. 29: © Bernard Gagnon, commons.wikimedia.org

pp. 30–33: courtesy of Thomas W. Davis

p. 37: © Evgeni, stock.adobe.com

p. 41: © Basak, commons.wikimedia.org

p. 45: © Pebo, stock.adobe.com

p. 53: Wellcome Library, London, wellcomeimages.org

p. 68: © Wilson44691, commons. wikimedia.org

p. 69: illustration from Richard Gilmour, *Bible History: Containing the Most Remarkable Events of the Old and New Testaments, with a Compendium of Church History* (1904)

p. 81: © David A. deSilva, Logos Bible Software (www.logos.com)

p. 85: © Renáta Sedmáková, stock.adobe.com

p. 94: © Ladislav Faigl, commons.wikimedia.org

p. 99: © Peter van der Sluijs, commons.wikimedia.org

p. 100: papyrus representation by Lydia Dahl; papyrus plant © little_airplane, stock.adobe.com

p. 101: University of Michigan Papyrology Collection, inventory number 6238

p. 104: © Christophe Jacquand, commons.wikimedia.org

p.139: Festus coin © Itamar, commons.wikimedia.org

p.151: © scaligar, stock.adobe.com

CONTRIBUTORS

MATTHEW D. AERNIE is associate professor of biblical studies for the College of Adult and Graduate Studies at Colorado Christian University. He is the coauthor of *The Righteous and Merciful Judge* (Lexham Press, 2018), which explores the significance of the concept of the "day of the Lord" for Paul's theology.

JOHN D. BARRY is the CEO of Jesus' Economy, an innovative nonprofit creating jobs and churches in the developing world. At JesusEconomy.org, people can shop fair trade and give directly to a cause they're passionate about, such as bringing the gospel to unreached people groups. John also is the general editor of *Faithlife Study Bible* and a past editor of *Bible Study Magazine*.

HOLLY BEERS teaches New Testament at Westmont College. Her publications include *The Followers of Jesus as the Servant: Luke's Model from Isaiah for the Disciples in Luke-Acts* (T&T Clark, 2015) and *A Week in the Life of a Greco-Roman Woman* (IVP Academic, forthcoming).

LYNN H. COHICK is provost at Denver Seminary and president of the Institute for Biblical Research. She researches the ways Jews and Christians lived out their faith in the ancient settings of Hellenism and the Roman Empire, and how Jews and Christians today can better appreciate and understand each other. Cohick is the author of the New Covenant Commentary on Ephesians (Cascade, 2010).

THOMAS W. DAVIS is professor of archaeology and biblical backgrounds at Southwestern Baptist Theological Seminary.

JOSEPH R. DODSON is associate professor of New Testament at Denver Seminary. Follow him on Twitter @jrrdodson.

TIMOTHY GOMBIS teaches New Testament at Grand Rapids Theological Seminary in Michigan.

JOSHUA W. JIPP is associate professor of New Testament at Trinity Evangelical Divinity School. He has written more extensively on hospitality to strangers in *Saved by Faith and Hospitality* (Eerdmans, 2017).

CRAIG S. KEENER is F. M. and Ada Thompson Professor of Biblical Studies at Asbury Theological Seminary. He is author of 28 books, seven of which have won awards, and over 100 academic articles and 200 popular-level articles.

BRIAN M. RAPSKE is professor of New Testament at Northwest Baptist Seminary, a member of the Associated Canadian Theological Schools (ACTS Seminaries) on the campus of Trinity Western University in Langley, British Columbia.

CARYN A. REEDER is professor of New Testament and department chair for religious studies at Westmont College. She is the author of *Gendering War and Peace in the Gospel of Luke* (Cambridge University Press, 2018).

RUTH ANNE REESE is professor of New Testament at Asbury Theological Seminary. She has written several books, including the Two Horizons Commentary on 2 Peter and Jude (Eerdmans, 2007).

E. RANDOLPH RICHARDS has authored or co-authored nine books and dozens of articles. He is currently working on *Rediscovering the New Testament* (IVP) and the Gospel of John volume in the Word Biblical Commentary series. He is provost and professor of biblical studies at Palm Beach Atlantic University.

ECKHARD J. SCHNABEL is the Mary F. Rockefeller Distinguished Professor of New Testament Studies at Gordon-Conwell Theological Seminary in South Hamilton, Massachusetts. He is the author of numerous books, commentaries, and essays, including *Early Christian Mission* and *Paul the Missionary,* and the associate editor of the Bulletin of Biblical Research.

DAVID B. SCHREINER is an assistant professor of Old Testament at Wesley Biblical Seminary in Jackson, Mississippi.

ANDREW SUTHERLAND is a PhD student in theological studies at Baylor University. He is a graduate of Duke Divinity School and a Bible study curriculum writer for Docent Research Group.

JAMES W. THOMPSON is scholar in residence at the Graduate School of Theology at Abilene Christian University in Abilene, Texas. He is the author of numerous books, including *Pastoral Ministry according to Paul: A Biblical Vision* (Baker Academic, 2006) and *The Church according to Paul: Rediscovering the Community Conformed to Christ* (Baker Academic, 2014).

SUSAN WENDEL is associate professor of New Testament at Briercrest College and Seminary in Saskatchewan, Canada. With the aim of serving the church, Susan studies, teaches, and writes in the areas of New Testament and early Christianity.

STEPHEN WITMER is a pastor and an adjunct professor of New Testament at Gordon-Conwell Theological Seminary in South Hamilton, Massachusetts. He is the author of *Eternity Changes Everything* and *Jonah: The Depths of Grace.*